THE MICROSOFT SETTLEMENT: A LOOK TO THE FUTURE

WEDNESDAY, DECEMBER 12, 2001

UNITED STATES SENATE,
COMMITTEE ON THE JUDICIARY,
Washington, DC.

The Committee met, pursuant to notice, at 10:08 a.m., in room SD–106, Dirksen Senate Office Building, Hon. Patrick J. Leahy, Chairman of the Committee, presiding.

Present: Senators Leahy, Kohl, Cantwell, Hatch, Kyl, DeWine, Sessions, and McConnell.

OPENING STATEMENT OF HON. PATRICK J. LEAHY, A U.S. SENATOR FROM THE STATE OF VERMONT

Chairman LEAHY. Good morning. I just want to do a little housekeeping here. I want to make sure the Chairman and Ranking Member of the Antitrust Subcommittee are here, Senator Kohl and Senator DeWine, both of whom have done a superb job for years in handling antitrust matters.

I told Senator DeWine earlier, and this will probably cause a recall petition from the Republican Party in Ohio, what a terrific job he did as Chairman and then what a terrific job Senator Kohl has done as Chairman on antitrust matters, and pointing out that they are issues of great complexity and great importance to everybody here in the Senate.

I have looked at the proposed settlement the Department of Justice and nine States have transmitted to the district court that is a plan for the conclusion of what has been really landmark antitrust litigation. But now it has got to pass the legal test set out in the Tunney Act if it is going to gain court approval, and that test is both simple and broad. It requires an evaluation of whether the proposed settlement is in the public interest.

There is significant difference of opinion over how well the proposed settlement passes this legal test. In fact, the States participating in the litigation against Microsoft are evenly split. Nine States joined in the proposed settlement and nine non-settling States presented the court with an alternative remedy.

As the courts wrangle with the technical and complex legal issues at stake in this case, this Committee is conducting hearings to educate ourselves, but also to educate the public about what this proposed settlement really means for our high-tech industry and for all of us who use computers at work and at school and at home.

Scrutiny of the proposed settlement by this Committee during the course of the Tunney Act proceeding is particularly important.

The focus of our hearing today is to examine whether the proposed settlement is good public policy and not to go into the legal technicalities. The questions raised here and views expressed may help inform the court. I plan, with Senator Hatch, to forward to the court the record of this hearing for consideration as the courts goes about the difficult task of completing the Tunney Act proceedings and the remedy sought by the non-settling States.

I am especially concerned that the district court take the opportunity seriously to consider the remedy proposal of the non-settling States, and to consider it before she makes her final determination on the other parties' proposed settlement. The insights of the other participants in this complicated and hard-fought case are going to be valuable additions to the comments received in the Tunney Act proceeding. I would hope they would help inform the evaluation whether the settlement is in the public interest, a matter which for many people is still an open question.

The effects of this case extend beyond simply the choices available in the software marketplace. The United States has long been the world leader in bringing innovative solutions to software problems, in creating new tools and applications for use on computers and the Web, and in driving forward the flow of capital into these new and rapidly growing sectors of the economy.

This creativity is not limited just to Silicon Valley. I think of my own home area, Burlington, Vermont. It ranks seventh in the Nation in terms of patent filings. Burlington is 38,000 people and it is in a county of about 130,000 people. This is not per-capita; this is actual filings—seventh in the Nation.

Whether the settlement proposal will help or hinder this process and whether the high-tech industries will play the important role they should in our Nation's economy is a larger issue behind the immediate effects of this proposal.

With that in mind, I intend to ask the representatives of the settling parties how their resolution of this conflict will serve the ends that the antitrust laws require. Our courts have developed a test for determining the effectiveness of a remedy in a Sherman Act case. The remedy must end the anticompetitive practices, it must deprive the wrongdoer of the fruits of the wrongdoing,and it must ensure that illegality never recurs. The Tunney Act also requires that any settlement of such a case serve the public interest.

Now, these are all high standards, but they are reasonable ones and people have dealt with them for years. In this case, the D.C. Circuit, sitting en banc and writing unanimously, found that Microsoft had engaged in serious exclusionary practices, to the detriment of their competitors, and thus to all consumers. So we have to satisfy ourselves that these matters have been addressed and redressed, or if they have not, why not.

I have noted my concern that the procedural posture of this case not jeopardize the opportunity of the non-settling States to have their day in court, and not deprive the district court of the value of their views on appropriate remedies in a timely fashion.

In addition, I have two basic areas of concern about the proposed settlement. First, I find many of the terms of the settlement to be either confusingly vague, subject to manipulation, or, worse, both. Mr. Rule raised an important and memorable point when he last

S. HRG. 107–772

THE MICROSOFT SETTLEMENT: A LOOK TO THE FUTURE

HEARING

BEFORE THE

COMMITTEE ON THE JUDICIARY
UNITED STATES SENATE

ONE HUNDRED SEVENTH CONGRESS

FIRST SESSION

DECEMBER 12, 2001

Serial No. J–107–53

Printed for the use of the Committee on the Judiciary

U.S. GOVERNMENT PRINTING OFFICE

82–938 PDF WASHINGTON : 2003

For sale by the Superintendent of Documents, U.S. Government Printing Office
Internet: bookstore.gpo.gov Phone: toll free (866) 512–1800; DC area (202) 512–1800
Fax: (202) 512–2250 Mail: Stop SSOP, Washington, DC 20402–0001

COMMITTEE ON THE JUDICIARY

PATRICK J. LEAHY, Vermont, *Chairman*

EDWARD M. KENNEDY, Massachusetts
JOSEPH R. BIDEN, JR., Delaware
HERBERT KOHL, Wisconsin
DIANNE FEINSTEIN, California
RUSSELL D. FEINGOLD, Wisconsin
CHARLES E. SCHUMER, New York
RICHARD J. DURBIN, Illinois
MARIA CANTWELL, Washington
JOHN EDWARDS, North Carolina

ORRIN G. HATCH, Utah
STROM THURMOND, South Carolina
CHARLES E. GRASSLEY, Iowa
ARLEN SPECTER, Pennsylvania
JON KYL, Arizona
MIKE DEWINE, Ohio
JEFF SESSIONS, Alabama
SAM BROWNBACK, Kansas
MITCH MCCONNELL, Kentucky

BRUCE A. COHEN, *Majority Chief Counsel and Staff Director*
SHARON PROST, *Minority Chief Counsel*
MAKAN DELRAHIM, *Minority Staff Director*

CONTENTS

STATEMENTS OF COMMITTEE MEMBERS

WITNESS

QUESTIONS AND ANSWERS

SUBMISSIONS FOR THE RECORD

CONTENTS

STATEMENTS OF COMMITTEE MEMBERS

WITNESS

QUESTIONS AND ANSWERS

SUBMISSIONS FOR THE RECORD

testified before this Committee in 1997 during the very important series of hearings that were convened by Senator Hatch on competition in the digital age, hearings that helped shape a lot of thinking in the Senate.

Testifying about the first Microsoft-Justice Department consent decree, Mr. Rule said, "Ambiguities in decrees are typically resolved against the Government. In addition, the Government's case must rise or fall on the language of the decree; the Government cannot fall back on some purported 'spirit' or 'purpose' of the decree to justify an interpretation that is not clearly supported by the language." So we take seriously such counsel. We would worry if ambiguity in the proposed settlement would jeopardize its enforcement.

Second, I am concerned that the enforcement mechanism described in the proposed decree lacks the power and the timeliness necessary to inspire confidence in its effectiveness. Particularly in light of the absence of any requirement that the decree be read in broad remedial terms, it is especially important that we inquire into the likely operation of the proposed enforcement scheme and its effectiveness.

Any lawyer who has litigated cases—and, Mr. James, that would certainly include you—and any business person knows how distracting litigation of this magnitude can be. We all appreciate the value that reaching an appropriate settlement can have not only for the parties, but also for consumers who are harmed by anti-competitive conduct, and the economy.

I am the first one to say we would like some finality so that everybody involved, all parties, can know what the standards are and all consumers can know what they are. Because of that, I don't come to this hearing pre-judging the merits of this proposed settlement, but instead as one who is ready to embrace a good settlement that puts an end to the merry-go-round of Microsoft litigation over consent decrees.

The serious questions that have been raised about the scope, enforceability and effectiveness of this proposed settlement leave me concerned that if it is approved in its current form, it may simply be an invitation for the next chapter of litigation.

I want an end to this thing. I think everybody wants an end to it, but we want an end to it where we know what the rules are going to be. If we don't know what the rules are going to be, as sure as the sun rising in the east we are going to face these issues again. On this point, I share the concern of Judge Robert Bork, who warns in his written submission that the proposed settlement "contains so many ambiguities and loopholes as to make it unenforceable and likely to guarantee years of additional litigation."

So I look forward to hearing from the Department of Justice and the other witnesses here. I will put into the record a series of letters: one, a letter to myself and Senator Hatch from James Barksdale; another, a letter to Assistant Attorney General James from Senator Hatch; a letter from Senator Hatch from Assistant Attorney General James; letters to myself and Senator Hatch from Robert Bork; a letter to myself from Ralph Nader, with two enclosures; written testimony of Catfish Software, Inc; and written testimony of Mark Havlicek of Digital Data Resources, Inc.

I yield to Senator Hatch, who did such superb hearings on this whole issue earlier.

STATEMENT OF HON. ORRIN G. HATCH, A U.S. SENATOR FROM THE STATE OF UTAH

Senator HATCH. Well, thank you, Mr. Chairman. As you know, we conducted a series of hearings, as you have mentioned, in this Committee in 1997 and 1998 to examine the policy implications of the competitive landscape of the then burgeoning high-tech economy and industry, which was about to explode with the advent of the Internet.

Those hearings focused on competition in the industry, in general, and more specifically on complaints that Microsoft had been engaged in anticompetitive behavior that threatened competition and innovation, to the detriment of consumers. Our goal was, and I believe today, is to determine how best to preserve competition and foster innovation in the high-technology industry.

Although the Committee and I, as its Chairman, was then criticized by some, I strongly believed then and continue to believe now that in a robust economy involving new technologies, effective antitrust enforcement today would prevent the need for heavy-handed Government regulation of business tomorrow.

My interest in the competitive marketplace in the high-technology industry was animated by my strong opposition to regulation of the industry, whether by government or by one or few companies. As we may remember, the hearings before the Judiciary Committee developed an extensive record of Microsoft's conduct and evidenced various efforts by the company to maintain and extend its operating system monopoly. These findings, I would note, were reaffirmed by a unanimous and ideologically diverse Court of Appeals. The Microsoft case and its ultimate resolution present one of the most important developments in antitrust law in recent history, certainly in my memory.

As I have emphasized before, having a monopoly is not illegal under our laws. In fact, in a successful capitalistic system, striving to be one should be encouraged, as a matter of fact. However, anticompetitive conduct intended to maintain or extend this monopoly would harm competition and could possibly be violative of our laws.

I believe no one would disagree that the D.C. Circuit Court's decision reaffirmed the fundamental principle that a monopolist, even a monopolist in a high-tech industry like software, must compete on the merits to maintain its monopoly, which brings us to today's hearing. We are here to examine the policy implications of the proposed settlement in the Government's antitrust litigation against Microsoft.

Mr. Chairman, rather than closing the book on the Microsoft inquiry, the proposed settlement appears to be only the end of the latest chapter. The settling parties are currently in the middle of the so-called Tunney Act process before the court, and the non-settling parties have chosen to further litigate this matter and last week filed their own proposed settlement. This has been a complex case with significant consequences for Microsoft, high-tech entrepreneurs, and the American public as well.

The proposed settlement between Microsoft, the Justice Department, and nine of the plaintiff State attorneys general is highly technical. We have all been studying it and its impact with great interest. Each of us has heard from some, including some of our witnesses here today, that the agreement contains much that is very good. Not surprisingly, we have also heard and read much criticism of the settlement. These are complex issues, and I would hope today's hearing will illuminate the many questions that we have.

I should note that about 2 weeks ago I sent a set of detailed and extensive questions about the scope, interpretation, and intended effects of the proposed settlement to the Justice Department, naturally seeking further information on my part.

First, I want to commend the Department for getting the responses to these questions to me promptly. We received them yesterday. I think the questions, which were made public, and the Department's responses could be helpful to each member in forming an independent and fair analysis of the proposed settlement.

To that end, and for the benefit of the Committee, Mr. Chairman, I would like to make both the questions and the Department's answers part of the record for this hearing. So I would ask unanimous consent that they be made part of the record.

As I noted in my November 29th letter to the Department, I have kept an open mind regarding this settlement and continue to do so. I have had questions regarding the practical enforceability of the proposed settlement and whether it will effectively remedy the unlawful practices identified by the D.C. Circuit and restore competition in the software marketplace.

I am also cognizant of both the limitation of the claims contained in the original Justice Department complaint by the D.C. Circuit, as well as the standards for enforcement under settled antitrust law. I believe that further information regarding precisely how the proposed settlement will be interpreted, given D.C. Circuit case law, is necessary to any full and objective analysis of the remedies proposed therein. I hope that this hearing will result in the development of such information that would supplement the questions that I have put forth to the Department.

Mr. Chairman, one important and critical policy issue that I would hope we can address today and that I would like all of our witnesses to consider, as they wait to be empaneled so that they can discuss, is the difficult issue of the temporal relation of antitrust enforcement in new high-technology markets.

It cannot be overemphasized that timing is a critical issue in examining conduct in the so-called "new economy." Indeed, the most significant lesson the Microsoft case has taught us is this fact. The D.C. Circuit found this issue noteworthy enough to discuss in the first few pages of its opinion, and I will quote from the unanimous court:

"[w]hat is somewhat problematic...is that just over 6 years have passed since Microsoft engaged in the first conduct plaintiffs allege to be anticompetitive. As the record in this case indicates, 6 years seems like an eternity in the computer industry. By the time a court can assess liability, firms, products, and the marketplace are likely to have changed dramatically. This, in turn, threatens enormous practical difficulties for courts considering the appropriate measure of relief in equitable enforcement actions." The court goes on to say, "Innovation to a large degree has already rendered the anticompetitive conduct obsolete (although by no means harmless)."

Now, this issue is one that is relevant for this Committee to consider as a larger policy matter, as well as how it relates to this case and the proposed settlement we are examining today.

Let me just say that one of the things that worries me is what are the enforcement capabilities of this settlement agreement? It was only a few years before these matters arose that Microsoft had agreed to a consent, a conduct decree that many feel they did not live up to. I think it is a legitimate issue to raise as to how will the agreement that the Justice Department has worked out with Microsoft and nine of the plaintiffs be enforced if anticompetitive conduct continues.

In that regard, let me just raise Mr. Barksdale's letter, which I believe you put into the record.

Chairman LEAHY. I did, I did.

Senator HATCH. Well, let me just raise it because he does make some interesting comments in his letter and I can read them, I think they might be at least part of opening up the questions in this matter. I will just quote a few paragraphs.

He says, "These developments have stiffened my resolve to do all I can to ensure that competition and consumer choice are reintroduced to the industry. It is vitally important that no company can do to a future Netscape what Microsoft did to Netscape from 1995 to 1999. It is universally recognized that the 1995 consent decree was ineffective. I respectfully submit that the Proposed Final Judgment, PFJ, which is the subject of the hearing, will be even less effective, if possible, than the 1995 decree in restoring competition and stopping anticompetitive behavior. Accordingly, Senator Leahy, I am going to follow your suggestion that I help the Committee answer one of the central questions. If the PFJ had been in effect all along, how would it have affected Netscape? More important, how will it affect future Netscapes?"

He describes the impact on future Netscapes as follows, and let me just read a couple of paragraphs in this regard. "As discussed in the attached document, the unambiguous conclusion is that if the PFJ agreed upon last month by Microsoft and the Department of Justice had been in existence in 1994, Netscape would have never been able to obtain the necessary venture capital financing. In fact, the company would not have come into being in the first place. The work of Mark Andreesen's team at the University of Illinois in developing the Mosaic browser would likely have remained an academic exercise. An innovative, independent browser company simply could not survive under the PFJ, and such would be the effect on any company developing in the future technologies as innovative as the browser was in the mid-1990's."

He goes on to characterize whether or not Microsoft could have developed this itself, but let me just read the last few paragraphs of this letter.

"If the PFJ provisions are allowed to go into effect, it is unrealistic to think that anybody would ever secure venture capital financing to compete against Microsoft. This would be a tragedy for our Nation. It makes a mockery of the notion that the PFJ is 'good for the economy' unquote. If the PFJ goes into effect, it will subject an entire industry to dominance by an unconstrained monopolist, thus snuffing out competition, consumer choice, and innovation in perhaps our Nation's most important industry. And, worse, it will allow them to extend their dominance to more businesses such as financial services, entertainment, telecommunications, and perhaps many others. Four years ago, I appeared before the Committee and was able to demonstrate, with the help of the audience, that Microsoft undoubtedly had a monopoly. Now, it has been proven in the courts that Microsoft not only has a monopoly, but they have illegally maintained that monopoly through a series of abusive and predatory actions. I submit to the Committee that Microsoft is infinitely stronger in each of their core businesses than they were 4 years ago, despite the fact that their principal arguments have been repudiated 8–0 by the Federal courts. I hope you will keep these thoughts in mind during your hearings." Then he said, "A more detailed analysis of my views follows."

Well, the importance of that letter is basically Barksdale was one of the original complainants against Microsoft and was one of the very important witnesses before this Committee in those years when we were trying to figure what we are doing here. I don't think you can ignore that, and so these questions have to be answered that he raises, plus the questions that I have given as well.

So you have put that letter in the record?

Chairman LEAHY. I have, and also I understood you wanted those letters that you had to Mr. James. Those are also part of the record.

Senator HATCH. I appreciate it.

Let me just say, Mr. Chairman, I am grateful that you are continuing the Committee's important role in high-technology policy matters, as I would expect you to do because I know that you take a great interest in these matters, as does, I think, every individual person on the Committee.

I certainly look forward to hearing our witnesses today, and I am going to keep an open mind on where we are going here. Hopefully we can resolve these matters in a way that is beneficial to everybody, including those who are against Microsoft and Microsoft itself.

Thank you, Mr. Chairman.

Chairman LEAHY. Thank you.

Senator Kohl?

STATEMENT OF HON. HERB KOHL, A U.S. SENATOR FROM THE STATE OF WISCONSIN

Senator KOHL. Mr. Chairman, we thank you for holding this hearing here today.

This is a crucial time for competition in the high-tech sector of our economy. After spending more than 3 years pursuing its groundbreaking antitrust case against Microsoft, the Government has announced a settlement. But the critical question remains, will this settlement break Microsoft's stranglehold over the computer software industry and restore competition in this vital sector of our economy? I have serious doubts that it will.

An independent Federal court, both the trial court and the Court of Appeals, found that Microsoft broke the law and that its violation should be fixed. This antitrust case was as big as they come. Microsoft crushed a competitor, illegally tried to maintain its monopoly, and stifled innovation in this market.

Now, after all these years of litigation, of charges and countercharges, this settlement leaves us wondering, did we really accomplish anything. Or in the words of the old song, "is that all there is?" Does this settlement obey the Supreme Court mandate that it must deny the antitrust violator the fruits of its illegal conduct?

It seems to me and to many, including nine of the States that joined the Federal Government in suing Microsoft, that this settlement agreement is not strong enough to do the job, to restore competition to the computer software industry. It contains so many loopholes, qualifications, and exceptions that many worry that Microsoft will easily be able to evade its provisions.

Today, for the vast majority of computer users, the first thing they see when they turn on their machine is the now familiar Microsoft logo, placed on the Microsoft start menu, and all of their computer operations take place through the filter of Microsoft's Windows operating system. Microsoft's control over the market is so strong that today more than 95 percent of all personal computers run on the Windows operating system, a market share high enough to constitute a monopoly under antitrust law.

Its share of the Internet browsing market is now over 85 percent, and it reported a profit margin of 25 percent in the most recent quarter, a very high number in challenging economic times. Microsoft has the power to dictate terms to manufacturers who wish to gain access to the Windows operating system and the ability to leverage its dominance into other forms of computer software. And Microsoft has never been shy about using its market power.

Are we today really confident that in 5 years this settlement will have had any appreciable impact on these facts of life in the computer industry? I am not.

We stand today on the threshold of writing the rules of competition in the digital age. We have two options. One option involves one dominant company controlling the computer desktop facing minor restraints that expire in 5 years, but acting as a gatekeeper to 95 percent of all personal computer users. The other model is the flowering of innovation and new products that resulted from the breakup of the AT&T telephone monopoly nearly 20 years ago. From cell phones to faxes, from long-distance price wars to the development of the Internet itself, the end of the telephone monopoly brought an explosion of new technologies and services that benefit millions of consumers everyday. We should insist on nothing less in this case.

In sum, any settlement in this case should make the market for computer software as competitive as the market for computer hardware is today. While there is nothing wrong with settling, of course, we should insist on a settlement that has an immediate, substantial and permanent impact on restoring competition in this industry.

I thank our witnesses for testifying today and we look forward to hearing your views.

Chairman LEAHY. Thank you.
Senator DeWine?

STATEMENT OF HON. MIKE DEWINE, A U.S. SENATOR FROM THE STATE OF OHIO

Senator DEWINE. Mr. Chairman, thank you very much for holding this very important hearing concerning the Department of Justice's Proposed Final Judgment in its case against Microsoft.

Mr. Chairman, as we examine this judgment and attempt to imagine what it will mean for the future of competition in this market, we must keep in mind the serious nature of this case. According to the D.C. Circuit Court, Microsoft did, in fact, violate our antitrust laws. Their behavior hurt the competitive marketplace. This is something that we must keep in mind as we examine the Proposed Final Judgment.

This hearing is particularly important at this time because Federal law does require the District Court to examine the proposed settlement and determine if it is, in fact, in the public interest. Federal law clearly allows the public to be heard on such matters. I believe that this forum today will further that process of public discussion.

The Court of Appeals in this case, relying on established Supreme Court case law, explained what an appropriate remedy in an antitrust case such as this one must seek to accomplish. It should unfetter the market from anticompetitive conduct, terminate the illegal monopoly, and deny the defendant the fruits of its violations. It is important, Mr. Chairman, that we examine whether the proposed decree would, in fact, accomplish these goals.

There seems to be a great deal of disagreement about what the competitive impact of the decree will be. While the proposed settlement correctly, I believe, focuses primarily on the market for middleware, there has been a great deal of concern raised about the mechanism for enforcing such a settlement. Specifically, I think we need to discuss further whether the public interest would be better served with a so-called special master or some sort of other administrative mechanism, or whether the Justice Department could be more effective enforcing the decree on its own.

In addition to the Department of Justice's Proposed Final Judgment, we also have the benefit of another remedies proposal that has been submitted to the court by nine States that did not join with the Antitrust Division's proposal. I would like to hear from our witnesses about the role they believe this alternative proposal should play in the ongoing Tunney Act proceedings.

As I mentioned earlier, Mr. Chairman, the Court of Appeals directed that any remedy should seek to deny Microsoft the fruits of its illegal activities. One clear benefit Microsoft derived from its violations was the effective destruction of Netscape as a serious competitor and a decrease in Java's market presence. It is obviously impossible to go back in time and resurrect the exact market structure that existed, but it is important to discuss how the proposed settlement deals with this problem.

I would also like to note for the record that Microsoft will be represented today by one of their outside counsels, Rick Rule, rather than an actual employee of the company. Mr. Rule is an outstanding antitrust lawyer. He is well qualified to testify on this issue and we certainly look forward to hearing his testimony today.

However, Mr. Chairman, I must say that I am disappointed that Microsoft chose not to send an actual officer of the company because it does not appear to represent, frankly, the fresh start that I think we were all hoping to begin today.

Finally, I would like to thank you, Mr. Chairman, Ranking Member Hatch, and Antitrust Subcommittee Chairman Kohl for all of your hard work in putting this hearing together and all of your work on this issue generally over the last few years.

I look forward to the testimony of our witnesses today and to the Committee's continuing oversight of this very important issue.

Chairman LEAHY. Mr. James, there is a vote on the floor. I think there are two or three minutes left in the roll call vote. We are going to suspend while we go to vote, but I think——

Senator MCCONNELL. Mr. Chairman, I have a really brief statement. Could I make that before you adjourn?

Chairman LEAHY. You can.

STATEMENT OF HON. MITCH MCCONNELL, A U.S. SENATOR FROM THE STATE OF KENTUCKY

Senator MCCONNELL. Let me just say that this hearing and the accompanying media spectacle indicate the Microsoft case is the subject of significant public interest and debate. Some argue that the case itself should never have been filed to begin with, and now after nearly 4 years of litigation, Microsoft, the Department of Justice and nine States have reached a settlement.

I just want to commend the parties for their tireless effort and countless hours spent in reaching the compromise. Settlement is nearly always preferable to litigation, and regulation by the market is nearly always better than regulation by litigation, or the Government for that matter.

As far as what the public thinks, just this week a nationwide survey indicated that the U.S. Government and Microsoft agreed to settle the antitrust case. However, nine State AGs argued that the antitrust case against Microsoft should continue. Which statement do you agree with?

The U.S. economy and consumers would be better off if the issue were settled as soon as possible: 70 percent. The court should continue to investigate whether Microsoft should be punished for its business activities: 24 percent. Not that the public is always determinative, but I thought that would be an interesting observation to add.

Thank you very much, Mr. Chairman.

Chairman LEAHY. Mr. James, I think you would note from the comments that they sort of go across the board here. The majority of people favor a settlement, but I must say that I don't think the majority of people favor any settlement; they favor a good settlement, and that is what the questions will be directed at and that is why nine attorneys general have expressed concern. Nine agreed with the settlement, nine disagreed with the settlement. These are all very good, very talented people. So in your testimony when we come back, you have heard a number of the questions that have been raised and we look forward to you responding to them.

We will stand in recess while we vote.

[The Committee stood in recess from 10:40 a.m. to 11:14 a.m.]

Chairman LEAHY. I should note for the record that Mr. James has served as the Assistant Attorney General for the Antitrust Division since June 2001. He previously served as Deputy Assistant Attorney General for the Antitrust Division for the first Bush administration from 1989 to 1992. He served as Acting Assistant Attorney General for several months in 1992, then was head of the antitrust practice at Jones, Day, Reavis and Pogue, in Washington.

Not knowing what the Senate schedule might be, Mr. James, we will put your whole statement in the record, of course. I wonder if you might summarize it, but also with some reference to the charge made in the letter to Senator Hatch and myself by Mr. Barksdale, who said had these been the ground rules, he never would have been able to get Netscape off the ground. Had these been the ground rules at the time they started Netscape, they never would have been able to create Netscape. If that is accurate, of course, then we have got a real problem.

So, Mr. James, it is all yours.

STATEMENT OF CHARLES A. JAMES, ASSISTANT ATTORNEY GENERAL, ANTITRUST DIVISION, DEPARTMENT OF JUSTICE, WASHINGTON, D.C.

Mr. JAMES. Thank you, Senator Leahy, and good morning to you and members of the Committee. I am pleased to appear before you today to discuss the proposed settlement of our still pending case against Microsoft Corporation.

With me today are Deborah Majoras, my deputy, and Phil Malone, who has been the lead staff lawyer on the Microsoft case from the very beginning. I note their presence here because they were the ones who responded to the judge's order that we negotiate around the clock and I think they have recovered now.

As you know, on November 2 the Department and nine States entered into the proposed settlement. We are in the midst of the Tunney Act period and that will end at the end of January, at which point the district court will determine whether the settlement is in the public interest. We think that it is.

I am somewhat limited in what I can say about the case because of the pendency of the Tunney Act proceeding. But, of course, I am happy to discuss this with the Committee for the purpose of public explication.

When thinking about the Microsoft case, from my perspective it is always important to distinguish between Microsoft, the public spectacle, and Microsoft, the actual legal dispute. We look, in particular, to what the Department alleged in its complaint and how the court ruled on those allegations.

The Antitrust Division's complaint had four counts: attempted monopolization of the browser market, in violation of Section 2; individual anticompetitive acts and a course of conduct to maintain the operating system monopoly, in violation of Section 2 of the Sherman Act; tying the own browser to the operating system, in violation of Section 1; and exclusive dealing, in violation of Section 1.

I would note that a separate monopoly leveraging claim brought by the States was thrown out prior to trial, and that the States at one time had alleged in their complaint monopolization of the Microsoft Office market. That was eliminated by the States through an amendment.

There was, of course, a trial before Judge Jackson, at the conclusion of which Judge Jackson found for the Government on everything but exclusive dealing. He ordered Microsoft to be split into separate operating system and applications businesses after a 1-year transitional period under interim conduct remedies.

On appeal, however, only the monopoly maintenance claim survived unscathed. The attempted monopoly claim was dismissed. The tying claim was reversed and remanded for further proceedings under a much more rigorous standard. And the remedy was vacated, with the court ordering remedial hearings before a new judge to address the fact that the liability findings had been, in their words, "drastically curtailed."

Even the monopoly maintenance claim was cut back in the Court of Appeals decision. The Court of Appeals found for Microsoft on some of the specific practices and ruled against the Government on the so-called course of conduct theory of liability.

I recount all of this history to make two basic points that I think are important as we discuss the settlement. First, the case, even as initially framed by the Department of Justice, was a fairly narrow challenge. It was never a direct assault on the acquisition of the operating system monopoly itself.

Second, and perhaps much more important, the case that emerged from the Court of Appeals was much narrower still, focusing exclusively on the middleware threat to the operating system monopoly and specific practices—not a course of conduct found to be anticompetitive.

The Court of Appeals decision determined the reality of the case as we found it in the Department when I first arrived there in June, as you noted. The conduct found to be unlawful by the court was the sole basis for relief.

It is probably worth talking just briefly about the monopoly maintenance claim. The complaint alleges that Microsoft engaged in various anticompetitive practices to impede the development of rival Web browsers and Java. These products came to be known as middleware and were thought to pose a threat to the operating system monopoly because they had the potential to become platforms for other software applications. The court noted that the middleware threat was nascent; that is to say that no one could predict when, if ever, enough applications would be written to middleware for it to significantly displace the operating system monopoly.

A few comments about the settlement itself. In general terms, our settlement has several important points that we think fully and demonstrably remedy the middleware issues that were at the heart of the monopoly maintenance claim.

In particular, our decree contains a very broad definition of middleware that specifically includes the forms of platform software that have been identified as potential operating system threats today and likely to emerge as operating system threats in the future. It prohibits in the broadest terms the types of contractual restrictions and exclusionary arrangements the Court of Appeals found to be unlawful. It fences in those prohibitions with appropriate non-discrimination and non-retaliation provisions, and it creates an environment in which middleware developers can create programs that compete with Microsoft on a function-by-function basis through a regime of mandatory API documentation and disclosure.

In the most simple terms, we believe our remedy will permit the development and deployment of middleware products without fear of retaliation or economic disadvantage. That is what we believe and what the court found that consumers actually lost through Microsoft's unlawful conduct, and that is what we think consumers will gain through our remedy.

With specific reference to what Mr. Barksdale said, if I may, I have not reviewed Mr. Barksdale's letter. I know that in this particular situation, with so much at stake in this particular settlement, I have seen lots of hyperbolic statements. I certainly wouldn't necessarily characterize his in that vein without having read it in some detail.

I would note, however, that——

Chairman LEAHY. Mr. James, we are going to give you an opportunity to do that because I want you to look at it. You can feel free to call it hyperbolic or however, but I would ask that you and your staff look at his letter, which does raise some serious questions, and I would like to see what response you have for the record.

Mr. JAMES. I would be happy to do so. And with that, I would be happy to answer your questions.

[The prepared statement of Mr. James follows.]

PREPARED STATEMENT OF CHARLES A. JAMES, ASSISTANT ATTORNEY GENERAL, ANTITRUST DIVISION, DEPARTMENT OF JUSTICE, WASHINGTON, D.C.

Mr. Chairman and members of the Subcommittee, I am pleased to appear before you today to discuss the Department's still-pending antitrust enforcement action against Microsoft Corporation.

On November 2, 2001, the Department stipulated to entry of a proposed consent decree that would resolve the case. Nine states joined in the proposed settlement.[1] We are in the midst of the 60-day public comment period under the Tunney Act, after which we will file a response to the comments, and the district court will rule on whether the proposed consent decree is in the public interest. Nine other states, and the District of Columbia, have not signed the proposed consent decree.

The Department's position regarding the proposed settlement is set forth in documents filed in the pending Tunney Act proceeding. Because of the pendency of the proceeding, and the somewhat remote possibility that the case will return to litigation, I am somewhat limited in what I can say about the case and settlement. Nonetheless, I am happy to appear before you today to dicuss in general terms how the settlement promotes the public interest by resolving the allegations sustained by the court of appeals.

When we in the Department address the MIcrosoft case, it is important for us to ignore the media spectacle and clash-of-the-titans imagery and focus instead on the actual legal dispute presented to the court. In discussing the case and the proposed consent decree, it is important to keep in mind not only what the Department alleged in our complaint, but how the courts—in particular, the D.C. Circuit—ruled. As a result of the appeals court's ruling, the case is in many important respects considerably narrower than the one the Department originally brought in the spring of 1998 and narrower still than Judge Jackson's ruling in June of 2000.

---

[1] New York, Ohio, Illinois, Kentucky, Louisiana, Maryland, Michigan, North Carolina, and Wisconsin

I would like to take a few minutes to refocus attention on the legal allegations charged in the complaint, how those allegations were resolved in the courts, and the remedies in the proposed consent decree presently undergoing Tunney Act review. I believe these proposed remedies fully and demonstrably resolve the monopoly maintenance finding that the D.C. Circuit affirmed.

The complaints filed by the Department, the states, and the District of Columbia alleged: (1) that Microsoft had engaged in a series of specific anticompetitive acts, and a course of anticompetitive conduct, to maintain its monopoly position in the market for operating systems designed to run on Intel-compatible personal computers, in violation of Section 2 of the Sherman Act; (2) that Microsoft had attempted to monopolize the web browser market, also in violation of Section 2; (3) that Microsoft had illegally tied its web browser, Internet Explorer, to its operating system, in violation of Section 1; and (4) that Microsoft had entered into exclusive dealing arrangements that also violated Section 1. A separate monopoly leveraging claim advanced by the state plaintiffs was dismissed prior to trial. After a full trial on the merits, the district court ultimately sustained the first three claims, while finding that the exclusive dealing claim had not been proved.

The D.C. Circuit, however, significantly narrowed the case, affirming the district court's finding of liability only as to the monopoly maintenance claim, and even there only as to a smaller number of specified anticompetitive actions. Of the twenty anticompetitive acts the court of appeals reviwed, it reversed with respect to eight of the acts that the district court had sustained as elements of the monopoly maintenance claim. Additionally, the D.C. Circuit reversed the lower court's finding that Microsoft's "course of conduct" separately violated Section 2 of the Sherman Act. It reversed the district court's ruling on the attempted monopolization and tying claims, remanding the tying claim for further proceedings under a much more difficult rule of reason standard. And, of course, it vacated the district court's final judgment that had set forth the break-up remedy and interim conduct remedies.

The antitrust laws do not prohibit a firm from having a monopoly, but only from illegally acquiring or maintaining a monopoly through interference with the competitive efforts of rivals. There has never been any serious contention that Microsoft *acquired* its operating system monopoly through unlawful means, and the existence of the operating system monopoly itself was not challenged in this case.

With regard to the monopoly maintenance claim, the court of appeals upheld the conclusion that Microsoft had engaged in unlawful exclusionary conduct by using contractual provisions to prohibit computer manufacturers from supporting competing middleware products on Microsoft's operating system; by prohibiting consumers and computer manufacturers from removing Microsoft's middleware products from the desktop; and by reaching agreements with software developers and third parties to exclude or disadvantage competing middleware products—all to protect Microsoft's monopoly in the operating system market.

The Department proved that Microsoft had engaged in these anticompetitive practices to discourage the development and deployment of rival web browsers and Java technologies, in an effort to prevent them from becoming middleware threats to its operating system monopoly. Netscape had gained a respectable market share as a technology for navigating the then-burgeoning Internet, and Netscape proponents were touting the prospect of a new world of Internet computing that would make operating systems less relevant. Netscape touted its web browser as a new category of software that came to be known as "middleware," a form of software that, like Microsoft's Windows operating system, exposed a broad range of applications program interfaces ("APIs") to which software developers could write applications. This created the potential that—if Netscape Navigator continued to gain market share and could run on operating systems other than Microsoft's, *and* if large numbers of software developers wrote applications programs to it—computer users would have viable competitive alternatives to Microsoft.

The middleware threat was nascent. That is, as both the district court and the court of appeals acknowledged, it was a potential threat to the operating system monopoly that had not yet become real. It could not be predicted when, if ever, enough applications programs would be written to middleware products for middleware to singificantly displace Microsoft operating systems. Microsoft took this nascent middleware threat to its operating system monopoly seriously. The trial record disclosed a corporate preoccupation with thwarting Netscape and displacing Netscape's Navigator with Microsoft's Internet Explorer as the prevailing web browser. This campaign featured a host of strong-arm tactics aimed at various computer manufacturers, Internet access providers, and independent software developers. Even the decision to integrate its own browser into the operating system—in effect, giving it away for free—had an element of impeding the growth of Netscape and once was described as taking away Netscape's oxygen. Microsoft took similar actions against

Java technologies. Among other things, Microsoft required software developers to promote its own version of Java technology exclusively and threatened developers if they assisted competing Java products.

The district court ruled not only that Microsoft had engaged in various specified illegal exclusionary practices, but that these acts were part of an overall anticompetitive course of conduct. The D.C. Circuit agreed as to some of the specified practices, while ruling that others—for example, Microsoft's practice of preventing computer manufacturers from substituting their own user interfaces over the Windows interface supplied by Microsoft—were justified and thus lawful. The D.C. Circuit also rejected the course-of-conduct theory, under which Microsoft's specific practices could be viewed as parts of a broader, more general monopolistic scheme, ruling that Microsoft's practices must be viewed individually.

Following the appellate court's instructions, we, in considering a possible remedy, focused on the specific practices that the court had ruled unlawfull. We took as a starting point the district court's interim conduct remedies. Those remedies, however, were based on a much wider range of liability findings than had been affirmed on appeal. Accordingly, they had to be tailored to the findings that had actually been affirmed. Further, because the interim conduct remedies were designed to apply only as a stop-gap until the district court's divestiture order was implemented, we broadened them in important respects to more fully address the remedial objectives of arresting the anticompetitive conduct, preventing its recurrence, and restoring lost competition to the marketplace. Finally, we updated the remedies to strengthen their long-term effectiveness in the face of the rapid technological innovation that continues to characterize the computer industry—so that they will be relevant to the Windows XP operating system world and beyond.

Under the proposed consent decree, Microsoft will be required to disclose to other software developers the interfaces used by Microsoft's middleware to interoperate with the operating system, enabling other software developers to create competing products that emulate Microsoft's integrated functions. Microsoft will also have to disclose the protocols that are necessary for software located in a server computer to interoperate with Windows on a PC.

Microsoft will have to permit computer manufacturers and consumers to substitute competing middleware software on the desktop. It will be prohibited from retaliating against computer manufacturers or software developers for supporting or developing certain competing software. To further guard against possible retaliation, Microsoft will be required to license its operating system to key computer manufacturers on uniform terms for five years.

Microsoft will be prohibited from entering into agreements rerquiring the exclusive support or development of certain Microsoft software, so that software developers and computer manufacturers can continue to do business with Microsoft while also supporting and developing rival middleware products. And Microsoft will be required to license any intellectual property to computer manufacturers and software developers necessary for them to exercise their rights under the proposed decree, including, for example, using the middleware protocols disclosed by Microsoft to interoperate with the operating system.

Any assumption that, had we litigated the remedy, we were certain to have secured all of this relief and possibly more misses the mark. The middleware definition, for example, was a very complex issue and would have been hard fought in a litigated remedy proceeding. The term had no generally accepted industry or technical meaning. At the time of trial, the term was used to describe software programs that exposed APIs. But in today's world, by virtue of the extensive degree to which software programs interact with each other, a very broad range of programs—large and small, simple and complex—expose APIs. At the same time, middleware had to be defined more broadly than the browser, or it would not provide sufficient protection for the potential sources of competition that might emerge. So we developed a definition of middleware, designed to encompass all technologies that have the potential to be middleware threats to Microsoft's operating system monopoly. It captures, in today's market, Internet browsers, e-mail client software, networked audio/video client software, and instant messaging software. On a going-forward basis, it also provides guidelines for what types of software will be considered middleware for purposes of the decree in the future. These guidelines are critical because, while it is important that future middleware products be captured by the proposed decree, those products will not necessarily be readily identified as such.

The proposed decree protects competition in the middleware market through a variety of affirmative duties and prohibition, which I listed a minute ago. By requiring disclosure of a broad range of interfaces and protocols that will secure interoperability for rival software and servers, broadly banning exclusive dealing, giving computer manufacturers and consumers extensive control of the desktop and initial boot sequence, and prohibiting a broad range of retaliatory conduct, the proposed decree will require Microsoft to fundamentally change the way in which it deals with computer manufacturers, Internet access providers, software developers, and others.

These prohibitions had to be devised keeping in mind that Microsoft will continue for the foreseeable future to have a monopoly in the operating systems market. While we recognized that not all forms of collaboration between Microsoft and others in the industry are anticompetitive, and that some actually benefit competition, we drafted the non-discrimination and non-retaliation provisions broadly enough to prevent Microsoft from using its monopoly power to apply anticompetitive pressure in this fashion.

We concluded, particularly in light of intervening technological developments in the computer industry, that the remedial objective of restoring lost competition had to mean something different than attempting to restore Netscape and Java specifically to their previous status as potential nascent threats to Microsoft's monopoly. Attempting to turn back the hands of time would likely prove futile and would risk sacrificing important innovations that have moved the industry beyond that point. So we focused instead on the market as it exists today, and where it appears to be heading over the next few years, and devised a remedy to recreate the potential for the emergence of competitive alternatives to Microsoft's operating system monopoly through middleware innovations. With a reported 70,000-odd applications currently designed to run on Windows, the applications barrier to entry is quite formidable. The most effective avenue for restoring the competitive potential of middleware, we concluded, was to ensure that middleware developers had access to the technical information necessary to create middleware programs that could compete with Microsoft in a meaningful way—that is, by requiring Microsoft to disclose the APIs needed to enable competing middleware developers to create middleware that matches Microsoft's in efficiency and functionality.

API disclosure had apparently been a very difficult obstacle to resolution of the case at every stage. There had never been any allegation in the case that Windows was an essential facility, the proprietary technology for which had to be openly shared in the industry. So we are very pleased that we were able to secure this crucial provision in the proposed decree.

Similarly, the proposed decree goes beyond the district court's order in requiring Microsoft to disclose communications protocols for servers if they are embedded in the operating system, thereby protecting the potential for server-based applications to emerge as a competitive alternative to Microsoft's operating systems monopoly. Although the issue of Microsoft's potential use of its monopoly power to inhibit server-based competition was barely raised and never litigated in the district court, we believed it was an important concern to resolve in the final negotiations.

The proposed decree also requires Microsoft to create and preserve "default" settings, such that certain of Microsoft's integrated middleware functions will not be able to override the selection of a third-party middleware product, and requires Microsoft to create add/delete functionality to make it easier for computer manufacturers and users to replace Microsoft middleware functionality with independently developed middleware. These are other important respects in which, in light of intervening technological changes, the proposed decree goes beyond the relief contemplated in the district court's interim relief order. By giving middleware developers the means of creating fully competitive products, requiring the creation of add/delete functionality, and making it absolutely clear that computer manufacturers can, in fact, replace Microsoft middleware on the desktop, the decree will do as much as possible to restore the nascent threat to the operating system monopoly that browsers once represented.

The proposed decree contains some of the most stringent enforcement provisions ever contained in any modern consent decree. In addition to the ordinary prosecutorial access powers, backed up by civil and criminal contempt authority, this decree has two other aggressive features. First, it requires a full-time, on-site compliance team—complete with its own staff and the power to hire consultants—that will monitor compliance with the decree, report violations to the Department, and attempt to resolve technical disputes under the disclosure provisions. The compliance team will have complete access to Microsoft's source code, records, facilities, and personnel. Its dispute resolution responsibilities reflect the recognition that the market will benefit from rapid, consensual resolution of issues whenever possible, more so than litigation under the Department's contempt powers. The dispute resolution process complements, but does not supplant, ordinary methods of enforcement. Complainants may bring their inquiries directly to the Department if they choose.

The decree will be in effect for five years. It also contains a provision under which the term may be extended by up to two additional years in the event that the court finds that Microsoft has engaged in repeated violations. Assuming that Microsoft will want to get out from under the decree's affirmative obligations and restrictions as soon as possible, the prospect that it might face an extension of the decree should provide an extra incentive to comply.

Our practice with regard to enforcement is never influenced by the extent to which we "trust" a defendant. Rather, a decree must stand on its own as an enforcement vehicle to ensure effective relief and must contain enforcement provisions sufficient to address its inherent compliance issues. In this case, those compliance issues are complex, as the decree seeks to address Microsoft's interactions with firms throughout the computer industry. Under the circumstances, I believe the extraordinary nature of the decree is warranted.

Some have criticized the decree for not going far enough. Some have asked why we did not continue to pursue divestiture as a possible remedy. We had several reasons. First, the court of appeals made it clear that it viewed the break-up remedy with skepticism, to put it mildly. The court ruled that on remand the district court must consider whether Microsoft is a unitary company—i.e., one that could not easily be broken up—and whether plaintiffs established a significant causal connection between Microsoft's anticompetitive conduct and its dominant position in the market for operating systems—a finding not reached by the prior judge.

Second, the legal basis for the structural separation the Department had been seeking was undercut by the failure to sustain the two claims that had challenged Microsoft's right to compete outside its operating system monopoly by integrating new functions into Windows, the attempted monopolization claim and the tying claim. The former was dismissed, and the latter was remanded under a much more difficult rule-of-reason standard. The court of appeals ruled that, albeit with some limits, Microsoft could lawfully integrate new functions into the operating system and use the advantages flowing from its knowledge and design of the operating system to compete in downstream markets.

Third, and more generally, the relief in a section 2 case must have its foundation in the offending conduct. The monopoly maintenance finding, as modified by the court of appeals, and without the "course-of-conduct" theory, would not in our view sustain a broad-ranging structural remedy that went beyond what was necessary to address Microsoft's unlawful responses to the middleware threat to its operating system monopoly. Indeed, our new district judge, Judge Kollar-Kotelly, stated in open court that she expected our proposed remedy to reflect the fact that portions of our case had not been sustained.

Finally, from a practical standpoint, even assuming that we could have eventually secured a breakup of Microsoft—a very dubious assumption in light of what the court of appeals and Judge Kollar-Kotelly have stated—the time it would have taken to continue litigating the break-up and the inevitable appeals could easily have delayed relief for another several years. By taking structural relief off of the table at the outset of the remedy proceeding on remand, we were able to get favorable procedural rulings that were essential to moving quickly to a prompt resolution.

More generally, a number of critics have suggested ways in which we could have further constrained Microsoft's conduct in the marketplace—either by excluding it from markets outside the operating system market, restricting it from integrating functions into its products or collaborating with others, or requiring it to widely share its source code as an open platform. While it is certainly true that restrictions and requirements of this sort might be desirable and advantageous to Microsoft's competitors, they would not necessarily be in the interest of competition and consumers overall; many would reduce consumer choice rather than increase it. Moreover, to the extent these restrictions go beyond what is needed to remedy proven antitrust violations, they are not legitimate remedial goals. The objectives of civil antitrust enforcement are remedial, and they focus on protecting and restoring competition for the benefit of consumers, not on favoring particular competitors.

As to more complex questions regarding whether the decree has properly covered all the elements that will be needed for full relief, questions of that nature are entirely appropriate and hopefully will be raised and addressed in the Tunney Act process.

But I believe the decree, by creating the opportunity for independent software vendors to develop competitive middleware products on a function by-function basis, by giving computer manufacturers the flexibility to place competing middleware products on Microsoft's operating system, and by preventing retaliation by Microsoft against those who choose to develop or use competing rniddleware products, fully addresses the legitimate public goals of stopping Microsoft's unlawful conduct and restoring competition lost on its account.

Mr. Chairman, a vigorously competitive computer software industry is vital to our economy, and the Department is committed to ensuring that it remains competitive.

I hope that my testimony has helped members of the Committee more fully understand why the Department is completely satisfied that the proposed consent decree now before the district court will provide a sufficient and effective remedy for the anticompetitive conduct in which Microsoft has been found to have engaged in violation of the Sherman Act. I would be happy to answer any questions you or other members of the Committee may have.

Chairman LEAHY. Did you have more that you wanted to say on the letter?

Mr. JAMES. No, sir. I am happy to respond to what you folks want to talk about.

Chairman LEAHY. The Department of Justice has been involved in litigation against Microsoft for more than 11 years. I am one of those who had hoped throughout that that the parties might come to some conclusion. I think that if you can have a fair conclusion, it is in the best interests of the consumers, the Government, Microsoft, competitors, and everybody else. I have no problem with that, but that presupposes the right kind of settlement.

Over the course of those 11 years, the parties entered into one consent decree that just ended up with a whole lot more litigation over the terms of that consent decree. I mention that because you take this settlement and it is already being criticized by some for the vagueness of its terms and its loopholes. Judge Robert Bork warned, and I think I am quoting him correctly, "It is likely to guarantee years of additional litigation."

Now, what kind of assurances can you give or what kind of predictions can you give that if this settlement is agreed to by the court that we are going to see an end to this litigation and we are going to have a stop to this kind of merry-go-round of Microsoft litigation concerning compliance or even the meanings of the consent decree?

I notice a lot of people in this room on both sides of the issue. I have a feeling that they are here solely because of their interest in Government and not because the meter is running. A lot of us would like to see this thing end, but why do you feel that this settlement is so good that that is going to end?

Mr. JAMES. Senator, that is certainly a legitimate question and I understand the spirit in which it is asked. One of the reasons that we have so many antitrust lawyers, and perhaps why there are so many of them in this room, is that firms with substantial market positions very often are the subject of appropriate antitrust scrutiny. So it is with Microsoft and so it should be.

Our settlement here is a settlement that resolves a fairly complex piece of litigation. By its terms it is going to be a complex settlement, inasmuch as it does cover a broad range of activities and has to look into the future prospectively in a manner that benefits consumers. And some of that consumer benefit certainly will come from the development of competing products. Some of that consumer benefit, however, will come from competition from Microsoft as it moves into other middleware products, et cetera.

We think that the terms of the decree are certainly enforceable. I think so much of what have been called loopholes are things that are carve-outs necessary to facilitate pro-competitive behavior. We certainly think that the enforcement power embodied in this decree—an unprecedented level of enforcement power with three tiers—is sufficient to let the Department of Justice do its job.

Chairman LEAHY. But keep in mind that usually in these kinds of decrees, if it is not specifically laid out, the courts tend to decide the vague questions against the Government, not for the Government. Fortune Magazine said even the loopholes have loopholes—a pretty strong statement from a very pro-business magazine. The settlement limits the types of retaliation Microsoft can take against PC manufacturers that want to carry or promote non-Microsoft software, but some would say that it gives a green light to other types of retaliation.

Now, why doesn't the settlement ban all types of retaliation? The Court of Appeals said twice that if you commingle the browser and operating system code, you violate Section 2 of the Sherman Act. The proposed settlement contains no prohibition on commingling code. There is no provision barring the commingling of browser code and the operating code. So you have got areas where they can retaliate. You don't have the barring of this commingling of code.

I mean, are Fortune Magazine, Judge Bork and others justified in thinking there are a few too many loopholes here, notwithstanding the levels of enforcement?

Mr. JAMES. Let me take your points in order. First, on the subject of retaliation, retaliation is a defined term in this decree. It is a term that we are using to define a sort of conduct that Microsoft can engage in when it engages in ordinary commercial transactions.

I don't think that there is any basis in the bounds of this case to prohibit Microsoft from engaging in any form of collaborative conduct with anyone in the computer industry. Certainly, the types of collaborative conduct that are permitted, the so-called loopholes, are the type of conduct that is permitted under standard Supreme Court law embodied in decisions like *Broadcast Music* and *NCAA*, and also embodied in the Federal Trade Commission-Department of Justice joint venture guidelines as sanctioned forms of conduct. So we think that antitrust lawyers certainly can understand these types of issues and we think the courts can understand these types of issues.

Secondly, with regard to your more particular point about commingling code, it is the case that the Court of Appeals, following upon the district court decision, found that Microsoft had engaged in an act of monopolization in that it commingled code for the purpose of preventing the Microsoft browser from being removed from the desktop. That is the finding of the Court of Appeals.

Now, in the process of going through my preparation for this hearing, I went back and looked at the Department of Justice's position with regard to this. Throughout the course of the case, and even in the contempt proceeding involving the former tying claims, it has always and consistently been the Department of Justice's contention that it did not want to force Microsoft to remove code from the operating system. They have said that over and over again in every brief that has been filed in this case.

What the Department of Justice wanted was an appropriate functionality that would give consumers the choice between middleware products. That is exactly the remedy that we have here and we think it is an effective remedy. We have gone beyond that particular aspect of this remedy by including in our decree a specific provision that deals with the questions of defaults—that is, the extent to which a non-Microsoft middleware product can take over and be invoked automatically in place of a Microsoft middleware product. That is something that was not in the earlier decrees. It is a step beyond what was included in Judge Jackson's order.

We think that we have addressed the product integration aspects of the Microsoft monopoly maintenance claim in exactly the terms that the Department has always pursued with regard to this particular issue, and we are completely satisfied with that aspect of the relief.

Chairman LEAHY. Well, I have a follow-up on that, as you probably expect, but my time is up and I want to yield to Senator DeWine. Actually, I have a follow-up on the retaliation, also, but I do appreciate your answer.

Senator DeWine?

Senator DEWINE. Thank you, Mr. Chairman.

Mr. James, this case has been certainly very controversial and inspired a great deal of discussion regarding the effectiveness of the antitrust laws, especially within the high-tech industry.

Netscape, for example, vocally opposed Microsoft during this litigation. Many of Netscape's complaints really were validated by the courts, and yet Netscape ended up losing the battle. This sort of result has led some to question whether our antitrust laws can be effective in this particular industry.

I personally believe that the antitrust laws are essential to promoting competition within the industry and throughout the country, but I would like to hear what your views are on this subject. What lessons do you think this case teaches us in regard to that and what do we say to people like Netscape?

Mr. JAMES. Well, it is certainly the case that our judicial system very often can provide a crude tool for redressing particular issues quickly. I would note that this particular case was litigated on a very fast track and the people at the Department of Justice are to be commended for pushing this case along at the speed that it is has taken, considering the comparable speed of other cases.

I think, however, that the case stands for an important proposition, and that is that the Department of Justice is up to meeting the challenge, that it has the tools at its disposal to investigate unlawful conduct, to understand and appreciate the implications of what complex technical matters involve, to bring the resources to bear in order to litigate these cases to a successful conclusion, and, where appropriate, to reach a settlement that is in the public interest.

One of the things that I think is an important issue to note here is that there is certainly a time difference between litigating a matter of original liability and litigating a matter involving compliance with a term of a decree.

We think that the enforcement powers that are involved here are appropriate ones. We think that enforcement by the Department of Justice is the appropriate way to proceed in these matters, and we are confident that this provides the best mechanism for dealing with a complex matter in complex circumstances.

Senator DEWINE. One provision of the Proposed Final Judgment requires Microsoft to allow computer manufacturers to enable access to competing products. However, for a product to qualify for these protections, it must have had a million copies distributed in the United States within the previous year. This would seem to me to run contrary to the traditional antitrust philosophy of promoting new competition.

Why are these protections limited to larger competitors?

Mr. JAMES. I am actually glad you asked that question, Senator, because that is one of the prevailing misconceptions of the decree. The provisions of the decree that require Microsoft to allow an OEM to place a middleware product on the desktop apply without regard to whether or not that product has been distributed by one million people. That is an absolute requirement.

The million-copy distribution provision relates solely to the question of when Microsoft must undertake these affirmative obligations to create defaults, for example, for a middleware product to provide other types of assistance to someone who has developed that product.

The fact of the matter is that this is something that requires a great deal of work, particularly these complex matters of setting defaults, which are very important to the competitive circumstances here. And it would be very difficult to impose upon Microsoft the responsibility for making these alterations to the operating system and making them automatic for every subsequent release of the operating system in the case of any software company that just shows up and says, "I have a product that competes."

But I want to be very clear here, Senator. An OEM can place every qualifying middleware product on the desktop immediately, without regard to this one-million threshold.

Quite frankly, in today's world, one million copies distributed is not a substantial matter. I think in the last year I might have gotten a million copies of AOL 5.0 in the mail. So I don't think that that is really a very large impediment.

Senator DEWINE. Let me ask one last question. You have mentioned that a number of provisions in the settlement go beyond the four corners of the case, but Microsoft agreed to these conditions anyway.

What are they, and what is the goal of these provisions?

Mr. JAMES. Well, I think one of the most important ones is the default provision. As of the time of our original case, these middleware products were operated in a fairly simple way. You clicked on to that product, you invoked that product, and then you used it in whatever way was appropriate.

In today's world, software has changed. We see what they call a more seamless user interface, user experience, and it is necessary for people to operate deeply within the operating system on an integrated basis. There were allegations that Microsoft overrode consumer choice in these default mechanisms in the case.

With regard to each and every one of those instances alleged by the Justice Department, the Justice Department lost. The court found for Microsoft. Notwithstanding that, as a matter of fencing in and improving the nature of this decree, we have included in it the subject of defaults.

Another important area, I think, is the question of server interoperability, and that is a very, very important issue we see going forward. If you go back and read the complaint in this case, you will find that the word "server" almost never appears. There are no specific allegations that go to this issue. We thought this was an important alternative platform issue. We thought it was important to stretch for relief in this case, and we got relief that is very effective as people go into an environment of more distributed Web processing. So we think that is a very powerful thing.

I think these are two issues that the Department of Justice would have had a very, very difficult time sustaining in court, to the extent the court was inclined to limit us to the proof that we put forward. So I think that these are very positive manifestations of the settlement.

Senator DEWINE. Thank you, Mr. Chairman.

Chairman LEAHY. We are checking one thing, and I mention this to Senator Kohl, Senator Sessions, and Senator Cantwell, who have been here waiting to ask questions. We are finding out from the floor. We have been notified that there may have been a move, as any Senator has a right to do under our Senate rules, to object to Committees meeting more than two hours after the Senate goes in session.

We are on the farm bill and appropriations and other essential matters, so that I have been told that a Senator has objected, as every Senator has a right to do, to us continuing. As a result, because the Senators say they want us to concentrate on what is going on on the Senate floor, we have to respect the rules of the Senate. I do, and I am going to have to recess this hearing at this time.

I am going to put into the record the statements of all those who have come here to testify.

Senator Hatch and I will try to find a time we might reconvene this hearing, because both Senator Hatch and I feel this is a very important hearing.

The record will be open for questions that might be submitted. I apologize to everybody. We did not anticipate this. But with 100 Senators, every so often somebody exercises that rule. I would emphasize Senators have the right to exercise that rule, especially when we are in the last 3 weeks of the session. I think we are going to break for Christmas Day, but we are in the last 3 weeks of the session, and I think the Senator invoking the rule wants to make sure all Senators pay attention to the work on the floor.

Senator HATCH. Mr. Chairman?

Senator SESSIONS. Mr. Chairman?

Chairman LEAHY. We really are technically out of time, but Senator Hatch?

Senator HATCH. Mr. Chairman, we are out of time. Any Senator can invoke the two-hour rule and a Senator has done that. Fortunately, I think it was against the Finance Committee markup today, but we reported out the bill anyway right within the time constraint. That is where I went.

Both Senator Leahy and I apologize to the witnesses who have put such an effort into being here today because this is an important hearing. These are important matters to both sides—to all sides, I should say; there are not just two sides here. These matters have a great bearing on just how positively impactful the United States is going to be in these areas.

So I hope that we can reconvene within a relatively short period of time and continue this hearing because it is a very, very important hearing. We apologize to you that this has happened, but as Senator Leahy has said, a Senator can do that.

Chairman LEAHY. Well, it is out of our hands, but I would note that normally I would have recessed it until tomorrow, but tomorrow we are using this time for an executive Committee meeting of the Judiciary Committee to do, as we have done many times already, to vote out a large number of judges.

So with that, we stand in—Jeff, I am sorry.

Senator SESSIONS. Just, Mr. Chairman, a matter of procedure. I am troubled by what I understand to be a decision to send this transcript to the court as an official document from Congress in the middle of a litigation that is ongoing.

I would think that anybody's statement that they gave could be sent to the court. Any Senator can write a letter to the court. I haven't studied it fully, but just as a practitioner, it troubles me to have a meddling——

Chairman LEAHY. That record is open to anybody who wants to send anything in. Senator Hatch and I have made that decision and that will be the decision of the Committee.

Senator SESSIONS. I would be recorded as objecting.

Chairman LEAHY. Of course, I understand.

We stand adjourned.

[Whereupon, at 11:43 a.m., the Committee was adjourned.]

[Questions and answers and submissions for the record follow.]

[Additional material is being retained in the Committee files.]

QUESTIONS AND ANSWERS

Responses of Daniel J. Bryant to questions from Senator Hatch

Question 1. An earlier decision by the Court of Appeals, *United States* v. *Microsoft Corp.*, 147 F.3d 935 (D.C.Cir. 1998) (*"Microsoft II"*), relating to the interpretation of an earlier consent decree with Microsoft, has been interpreted by some as expressing the view that judges should not be involved in software design, and that the government simply has no business telling Microsoft or any other company what it can include in any of its products. In its most recent decision, however, the Court of Appeals said that to the extent that the decision in *Microsoft II* completely disclaimed judicial capacity to evaluate high-tech product design, it cannot be said to conform to prevailing antitrust doctrine. *See United States v. Microsoft Corp.*, 253 F.3d 34 (D.C. Cir. 2001) (*"Microsoft III"*). Is the law clear that the Department does have a responsibility to assess the competitive implications of software design, in bringing antitrust enforcement actions? And, if so, does the Department have the necessary technical expertise and resources to perform such an evaluation?

Answer. In exercising its responsibility to enforce the antitrust laws, the Department routinely confronts complex issues, including economic and technical issues regarding software design. The Department has both the resources and capability to address such issues, as they affect enforcement matters, through internal means and, where appropriate, the retention of outside experts.

Question 2. To foster competition in "middleware" the PFJ requires disclosure of APIs and similar information, but it then limits this provision only to those instances where disclosure would be for "the sole purpose of interoperating with a Windows Operating System Product." Except for the limitation, this provision is almost exactly like a comparable provision in Judge Jackson's interim consent decree. Why did the Department decide to add this limitation to the PFJ, and what effect will the inclusion of the limitation have on restoring competition? Please explain the competitive significance of web-based services, and whether the PH guarantees interoperability with the servers that operate those web-based services?

Answer. The insertion of "for the sole purpose of interoperating with a Windows Operating System Product" in Section III.D. of the proposed Final Judgment simply clarifies that the APIs must be used for the purpose intended under the settlement (and as intended in Judge Jackson's order)—ensuring that developers of competing middleware products will have full access to the same information that Microsoft middleware uses to interoperate with the Windows operating system. That is, the disclosure is not intended to permit misappropriation of Microsoft's intellectual property for other uses. The insertion of this clause will not change the provision's ability to restore competition in any way.

The concept of "web-based" services is constantly evolving as companies find new ways. to use the Internet. The ultimate competitive significance of such services remains to be determined. The Department's case addressed the topic of web-based services only with respect to the middleware threat to the operating system. Section III.E. of the proposed Final Judgment ensures that software developers will have full access to, and be able to use, the communication protocols necessary for server operating system software located on a server computer to interoperate with the functionality embedded in the Windows operating system.

Question 3. The Department has concluded that the PFJ is in the "public interest," as required by the Tunney Act. Are you aware of any other case where a Tunney Act "public interest" determination has occurred with respect to a settlement where the underlying liability on the merits already has been affirmed by the Court of Appeals? To what extent should the scope of the District Court's deference to the Antitrust Division under the Tunney Act he affected by a Court of Appeals prior affirmance of Sherman Act liability?

Answer. The Department is not aware of a case where a court has made a Tunney Act "public interest" determination with respect to a settlement where the underlying liability on the merits already had been affirmed by the Court of Appeals. Beyond the Department's position set forth in its submissions to the Court, it would be inappropriate for the Department to comment on the appropriate scope of the Court's discretion because the Court's review of the proposed Final Judgment is pending under the Tunney Act.

Question 4. The Court of Appeals remanded the remedy issue because, among other reasons, the District Court failed to demonstrate how divestiture relief was designed to "'unfetter [the] market from anticompetitive conduct,'. . . to 'terminate the illegal monopoly, deny to the defendant the fruits of its statutory violation, and ensure that there remain no practices likely to result in monopolization in the future'" *Microsoft III*, 253 F.3d at 103 (quoting *Ford Motor Co. V. United States*, 405 U.S. 562, 577 (1972), *United States v. United Shoe Mach. Corp.*, 391 U.S. 244, 250 (1968)). Please describe how the PFJ meets this standard dictated by the appellate court. (a) How does the PFJ "terminate the monopoly" Microsoft was found by the Appellate Court to have unlawfully maintained over PC operating system software? (b) How does the PFJ "deny to Microsoft the fruits of its Section 2 violation?" and (c) How does the PFJ "ensure that there remain no practices likely to result in monopolization in the future?"

Answer. In the two cases quoted above, the monopoly in question was obtained by unlawful means. It was never alleged in this case, however, that Microsoft unlawfully *obtained* its operating system monopoly. Further, as the Court of Appeals noted, "the District Court expressly did not adopt the position that Microsoft would have lost its position in the OS market but for its anticompetitive behavior." *U.S. v. Microsoft*, 253 F.3d 34, 107 (D.C. Cir. 2001). The Court of Appeals also went on to hold that: "[s]tructural relief, which is 'designed to eliminate the monopoly altogether . . . require[s] a clear indication of a significant causal connection between the conduct and creation or maintenance of the market power.' Absent such causation, the antitrust defendant's unlawful behavior should be remedied by 'an injunction against continuation of that conduct.'" *Id.* at 106 (quoting 3 AREEDA&HOVENKAMP, ANTITRUST LAW ¶653b, at 91–92, and ¶650a, at 67). The injunctive relief in this case, with no allegation Microsoft unlawfully obtained its operating system monopoly, is designed to stop the unlawful conduct, prevent its recurrence and restore lost competition in the market. *See Microsoft*, 253 F.3d at 103 (quoting *Ford Motor Co. v. United States*, 405 U.S. 562, 577 (1972) and *United States v. United Shoe Mach. Corp.*, 391 U.S. 244, 250 (1968)).

The proposed Final Judgment stops the offending conduct by enjoining the unlawful actions that the District Court and the Court of Appeals sustained. The proposed Final Judgment enjoins exclusive and unlawful dealing, gives computer manufacturers and consumers extensive control of the desktop and initial boot sequence, ensures that developers can develop products that interoperate with the Windows operating system, and prohibits a broad range of retaliatory conduct. The proposed Final Judgment prevents the recurrence of the conduct identified as unlawful by addressing the broad range of potential strategies Microsoft might deploy to impede the emergence of competing middleware products. The proposed Final Judgment also seeks to restore lost competition posed by the potential middleware threat to Microsoft's operating system monopoly by requiring Microsoft to, among other things: (i) disclose APIs that will give independent software developers the opportunity to match Microsoft's middleware functionality; (ii) allow computer manufacturers and users to replace Microsoft middleware with independently developed middleware; and (iii) create and preserve "default" settings that will ensure that Microsoft's middleware does not over-ride the selection of third-party middleware products.

Question 5. Are there findings by the appellate court against Microsoft that are not addressed by the PFJ? If so, what were the reasons why the Department chose not to address these findings?

Answer. The proposed Final Judgment addresses each of the Court of Appeals' findings, and even goes beyond them.

Question 6. The Court of Appeals held that it was illegal for Microsoft to bind products together with Windows by "commingling code" because this practice helped Microsoft unlawfully maintain its desktop operating system monopoly. The Court concluded that code commingling has an "anticompetitive effect" by deterring OEMs from pre-installing rival software, "thereby reducing the rivals' usage share and, hence, developers' interest in rivals' APIs as an alternative to the API set exposed by Microsoft's operating system." *Microsoft III*, 153 F.3d at 66. How does the PFJ prevent Microsoft from future unlawful commingling of non-Windows code with Windows?

Answer. The proposed Final Judgment addresses these issues by requiring Microsoft to redesign its operating system to include an effective add/remove function for all Microsoft middleware products and to permit competing middleware to take on a default status that will override middleware functions Microsoft has integrated into the operating system. The proposed Final Judgment does not contain an absolute prohibition on Microsoft commingling code within Windows, and the Department does not interpret the Court of Appeals decision as requiring such relief.

Question 7. You have said that Microsoft "won the right to sell integrated products," and that "the tying claim was eliminated by the appeals court." (Business Week, November 19, 2001, p. 116). Other observers, however, argue that the Court of Appeals simply vacated the per se findings of a tying law violation and remanded that issue for consideration under a "rule of reason" standard? Why did the Department conclude that the tying claim was "eliminated" and not simply remanded to be retried under a different standard? What are the circumstances, if any, under which the court or the Department could find it impermissible for Microsoft to "integrate" a product with its Windows operating system?

Answer. The Court of Appeals reversed the per se tying claim and remanded it to the lower court for adjudication under a more rigorous legal standard. The Court also held that if the Department pursued the tying claim on remand it would be precluded from arguing any theory of harm relying on a precise definition of browsers or barriers to entry, even though the government would have the burden of showing an anticompetitive effect in the browser market. The Court of Appeals also invited an extensive and complex analysis of pricing, noting that other operating system manufacturers included Web browsers in their operating systems, and requiring the plaintiffs to show that any anticompetitive effects outweighed the procompetitive effects. In light of the Court's decision and the desire to achieve prompt relief for consumers without protracted litigation and appeals, the Department and the state plaintiffs decided not to pursue the tying claim.

Given the continuing pendency of this litigation and the possibility that these issues may arise in other contexts, it is not appropriate for the Department to speculate under what circumstances Microsoft's conduct would be impermissible.

Question 8. The CIS acknowledges that the "users rarely switched from whatever browsing software was placed most readily at their disposal." It has been suggested that the most effective way to restore competition and to prevent future misconduct would be to require Microsoft to sell a product that is simply an operating system without all of the various applications that are now incorporated into Windows. Without such a requirement, the argument goes, consumers would be forced to procure two products if they choose to use a non-Microsoft version of a product that has been included in the operating system—Microsoft's version and the competitor's version. If Microsoft middleware is preinstalled with Windows, how do you think the adoption rate by users of non-Microsoft middleware will be affected? Did the Department consider including in the PFJ a requirement that Microsoft sell a version of Windows that is solely an operating system without other applications bundled with it?

Answer. The Department did consider, and ultimately, reject a remedy that would have required Microsoft to sell a version of its operating system that did not contain some or all of the applications that it typically includes with the Windows operating system. First, this relief would have been most appropriate to remedy the tying and attempted monopolization liability (which were not sustained by the Court of Appeals), rather than for monopoly maintenance. Second, the remedy would reduce consumer choice rather than increase it. The proposed Final Judgment provides computer manufacturers the option of featuring, and end users the option of selecting, alternative middleware products, which they may choose to use or replace. Even if Microsoft middleware is preinstalled on the computer, computer manufacturers will have the ability to remove access to it and replace it with independently developed middleware. In this way, competition for consumer patronage of middleware products, unfettered by artificial restrictions by Microsoft, will determine adoption rates.

Question 9. Some observers claim the Court of Appeals found that Microsoft's technological tying, particularly its "commingling of code," was a1 illegal act of monopolization under Section 2 of the Sherman Act, but that there was insufficient evidence to determine that the same conduct violated Section 1. Do you agree with this? Does the PFJ provide a remedy for such misconduct? In your analysis, does the failure to find that the conduct violated Section 1 obviate the need to provide a remedy for the violation the court found under Section 2?

Answer. The Court of Appeals observed some overlap between the tying claim and the code integration issues under the monopoly maintenance claim. However, as the Court of Appeals noted, the District Court concluded that tying and commingling are two different things—"[a]lthough the District Court also found that Microsoft commingled the operating system-only and browser-only routines in the same library files, it did not include this as a basis for tying liability despite plaintiffs' request that it do so." *U.S. v. Microsoft*, 253 F.3d 34, 85 (D.C. Cir. 2001). The Department believes that the proposed Final Judgment effectively addresses the integration issues of the monopoly maintenance claim by requiring Microsoft to redesign its operating system to include an effective add/remove function for all Microsoft middleware products and to permit competing middleware to be featured in its place, as well as take on a default status that will, if the consumer chooses, override middleware functions Microsoft has integrated into the operating system.

Question 10. Some Wall Street analysts have opined that the PFJ imposes no obligation on Microsoft to change its business practices or redesign its products. Instead, these analysts have concluded, the PFJ seeks to restore competition by permitting OEMs to add products to Microsoft's desktop. Is this view of the PFJ accurate? Is it the Department's position that OEMs are in the best economic position to restore competition in personal computing? If so, what is the basis for that position? Are there other entities that might be in a position to help restore competition?

Answer. The Department fundamentally disagrees with this characterization of the proposed Final Judgment. The proposed Final Judgment will require Microsoft to fundamentally change the way in which it deals with computer manufacturers, Internet access providers, software developers and others within the computer industry with regard to the manner in which it designs, sells, and shares information regarding its operating system. The proposed Final Judgment does not reflect a position by the Department that computer manufacturers are the only distribution outlet for software or that they are the only ones in a position to help restore competition. In fact, consumers increasingly obtain software in various distribution channels apart from computer manufacturers. Rather, certain provisions in the proposed Final Judgment focus on computer manufacturers because the restrictions on computer manufacturers to distribute software was a primary focus of the case and the Court of Appeals concluded that computer manufacturers were a critical distribution channel for Windows, as well as for middleware and other software applications.

Question 11. A significant portion of the *Microsoft III* opinion was devoted to Microsoft's conduct vis-a-vis Java technology. The Court found Microsoft unlawfully used distribution agreements to forestall competition with middleware manufacturers. *See, e.g., Microsoft III*, 253 F.3d at 74–78. The court found these agreements to be anticompetitive because they "foreclosed a substantial portion of the field for . . . . distribution and because, in so doing, they protected Microsoft's monopoly from a middleware threat" *Id. at 76*. Does the PFJ addressees such practices?

Answer. The proposed Final Judgment addresses such conduct by prohibiting Microsoft from entering into agreements that require software developers and other industry participants to exclusively distribute, promote, use or support a Microsoft middleware or operating system product, and by prohibiting Microsoft from retaliating against software developers who support competing middleware products.

Question 12. The Supreme Court has said that in an antitrust remedy, "it is not necessary that all of the untraveled roads to that [unlawful] end be left open and that only the worn one be closed." *International Salt Co. v. United States*, 332 U.S. 392, 401 (1947). The Court also has made clear that injunctive relief which simply forbid[s] a repetition of the illegal conduct is not sufficient under Section 2, because defendants "could retain the full dividends of their monopolistic practices and profit from the unlawful restraints of trade which they had inflicted on competitors." *Schine Chain Theaters, Inc. v. United States*, 334 U.S. 110, 128 (1948). Are the standards enunciated by the Court in *International Salt and Schine Chain Theatres* applicable in the Microsoft case? If so, would you identify provisions in the PFJ that satisfy these standards?

Answer. The obligations imposed on Microsoft in the proposed Final Judgment go considerably beyond merely stopping, and preventing the recurrence of, the specific acts found unlawful by the Court of Appeals. Specifically, the proposed Final Judgment goes further by: (i) applying a broad definition of middleware products, which goes well beyond the Web browser and Java technologies that were the focus of the Department's case, to include all of the technologies that have the potential to be middleware threats to Microsoft's operating system monopoly, including e-mail clients, media players, instant messaging software and future middleware developments; (ii) requiring the disclosure or licensing of middleware interfaces and server communications protocols not previously disclosed to ensure that non-Microsoft middleware and server software can interoperate with Microsoft's operating system; (iii) ensuring that computer manufacturers and consumers have extensive control of the desktop and initial boot sequence; (iv) broadly banning certain exclusive dealing, retaliation and discrimination by Microsoft beyond the practices affirmed as anticompetitive by the Court of Appeals; (v) requiring Microsoft to license its operating system to key computer manufacturers on uniform terms; (vi) requiring Microsoft to license intellectual property to computer manufacturers and software developers necessary for them to exercise their rights under the proposed settlement; and (vii) implementing a panel of three independent, on-site, full-time experts to assist in enforcing the proposed Final Judgment.

Question 13. The Supreme Court also has held that a Section 2 monopolization remedy "must break up or render impotent the monopoly power found to be in violation of the Act." *United States v. Grinnelll Corp.*, 384 U.S. 563, 577 (1966). Does the PFJ "render impotent" Microsoft's Windows monopoly and, if so, how?

Answer. In the case against Microsoft there has never been any contention that Microsoft *obtained* its operating system monopoly through unlawful means. Instead, the allegation sustained by the Court of Appeals was that Microsoft engaged in specific unlawful acts, not a course of conduct, to *maintain* its monopoly in violation of Section 2. Because relief in a Section 2 case must have its foundation in the offending conduct, the Department's view was that the monopoly maintenance finding, as modified by the Court of Appeals, and without the "course-of-conduct" theory, did not sustain a broad-ranging remedy, such as a "break up" of Microsoft's operating system monopoly, that went beyond what was necessary to address Microsoft's unlawful responses to the middleware threat. Thus, the proposed Final Judgment does not seek such break-up relief.

Question 14. There has been considerable discussion about Microsoft's Windows XP product, with some critics arguing that Microsoft is repeating the same technical binding, bundling and monopoly maintenance tactics found by the court to be unlawful when used in the past against Microsoft's competitors. If true, this allegation would be significant, given the appellate court's instruction "that there remain no practices likely to result in monopolization in the future," *Microsoft III*, 253 F.3d at 103 (quoting *United States v. United Shore Mach. Corp.*, 391 U. S. 244, 250 (1968)). Some critics have also charged that Microsoft's broad .NET strategy is an effort to build upon the fruits of Microsoft's past unlawful conduct and remake the Internet as a Microsoft-proprietary Internet. Does the PFJ apply to Windows XP or to Microsoft's .NET strategy? If not, why has the Department decided not to apply the settlement to these products? Can competition in the operating system be restored without addressing these products?

Answer. With the monopoly maintenance claim as the only surviving basis for relief, the proposed Final Judgment must focus on middleware or middleware-type threats to the operating system, not Microsoft's participation in other markets in a way unrelated to the conduct by Microsoft found unlawful by the Court of Appeals. The proposed Final Judgment expressly applies to Windows XP and any successors during the term of the judgment (see definition of Windows Operating System Product). It also applies to a wide variety of current and future Microsoft middleware products. What has been labeled.NET is a relatively new, diverse initiative by Microsoft in the market. As parts of.NET come more fully to fruition, they will be evaluated under the proposed Final Judgment, as would any other software. For instance, parts of the.NET strategy are likely to be middleware, such as instant messaging clients. To the extent.NET software or conduct implicates the anticompetitive acts raised in the case, it would be addressed under the proposed Final Judgment or otherwise by the Department.

Question 15. Many of the provisions of the PFJ appear to assume that OEMs will act to aggregate operating system software and assume the role of desktop design and software packaging in the PC distribution chain. According to many observers, however, there simply is no financial incentive for OEMs to do anything but accept the full Microsoft software package. What is the Department's position on this issue? Was any consideration given to reports that OEMs did not take advantage of an offer by Microsoft this past summer to replace icons in the Windows Xf desktop?

Answer. During the trial, the Department showed, and the Court of Appeals found, that computer manufacturers are a key distribution channel for Windows, as well as for middleware and other software applications. Further, even before the proposed Final Judgment was executed, computer manufacturers were entering into agreements with non-Microsoft middleware suppliers to place their products on the Windows operating system. With the implementation of the proposed Final Judgment, which provides computer manufacturers with greater freedom with respect to replacing Microsoft middleware products, computer manufacturers should have even greater incentives to do so. The powers extend well beyond the limited rights Microsoft afforded when Windows XP was introduced this past summer. The true test will occur as the uncertainty surrounding the case is removed by the proposed Final Judgment, when the proposed Final Judgment's anti-retaliation and anti-discrimination terms are in place, and when new middleware products emerge on the market.

Question 16. The Court of Appeals affirmed that Microsoft's conduct with respect to Java, in which the Court found it to engage in a "campaign to deceive [Java] developers" and "polluted" the Java standard in order to defeat competition to its operating system monopoly violated Section 2 of the Sherman Act. The Court held "Microsoft's conduct related to its Java developer tools served to protect its monopoly of the operating system in a manner not attributable either to the superiority of the operating system or to the acumen of its makers, and therefore was anticompetitive. Unsurprisingly, Microsoft offers no procompetitive explanation for its campaign to deceive developers. Accordingly, we conclude this conduct is exclusionary, in violation of Section 2 of the Sherman Act." *Microsoft III*, Slip Op. p. 101. As you know, the lower court decree included a provision designed to prevent deliberate sabotaging of competing products by Microsoft. Does the PFJ restrict Microsoft's ability to modify, alter, or refuse to support computer industry standards, including Java, or to engage in campaigns to deceive developers of competitor platform, middleware or applications software?

Answer. The proposed Final Judgment does not expressly restrict Microsoft's ability to modify, alter, or refuse to support computer industry standards, or engage in campaigns to deceive software developers. The Department chose not to include the referenced provision because the term originally included in Judge Jackson's order allowed Microsoft to take steps to change its operating system that would interfere with third-party's middleware to interoperate as long as Microsoft informed the third party of the change and what, if anything, could be done to fix the problem. This would have, in effect, given Microsoft a license to interfere with competing middleware as long as it simply notified the competing developer. In addition, this provision would have been difficult for the Department to enforce in this case because of the constant changes Microsoft makes to its operating system, which while potentially procompetitive, may have the unintentional consequence of affecting a competing product's interoperability. Therefore, implementing this provision would have resulted in unnecessary compliance disputes.

The proposed Final Judgment hinders Microsoft's ability to disadvantage competing middleware developers by making the means by which middleware products interoperate with the operating system more transparent. The proposed Final Judgment requires Microsoft to now disclose those APIs that its middleware products use to interoperate with the operating system. Disclosure of these APIs will make it harder for Microsoft to interfere with competing middleware. Further, to the extent computer industry standards are implemented in communications protocols, as often occurs, Microsoft must license those protocols in accordance with Section III.E., including any modifications or alterations to the industry standard protocols. When the industry standard is implemented between a Microsoft middleware product, such as its Java Virtual Machine, and the operating system, Microsoft must disclose that interface.

Question 17. The Court of Appeals found that Microsoft violated Section 2 of the Sherman Act by entering into an exclusive contract with Apple that required Apple to install Internet Explorer as the Macintosh browser. *Microsoft III*, 252 F.3d at 72–74. Many observers accuse Microsoft of having forced Apple to enter into the contract by threatening to withhold the porting of Microsoft Office to the Macintosh operating system. Does the PFJ prohibit Microsoft from threatening to withhold development of Microsoft Office with respect to other platforms, such as hand-held devices, set-top boxes, and phones? If no, why did the Department choose not to address this concern in the PFJ?

Answer. The proposed Final Judgment would prohibit Microsoft from threatening to withhold the development of Microsoft Office for other platforms, such as handheld devices, set-top boxes and phones, if it did so because the software or hardware developer was developing, using, distributing, promoting or supporting any software that competes with Microsoft's middleware or operating system products (or any software that runs on any software that competes with Microsoft's middleware or operating system products), or because the developer exercises any of the options or alternatives provided for under the proposed Final Judgment.

Question 18. You have been quoted as saying that various software and computer services companies are in the process of purchasing space on the desktop from Microsoft. (Business Week, November 19, 2001, p. 116). In the Department's view, is the space on the desktop on computers manufactured by the OEMs owned by Microsoft or should that space be the property of the computer manufacturers?

Answer. Whether the space on the desktop is owned by Microsoft or is the property of the computer manufacturers does not impact the effectiveness of the proposed Final Judgment in remedying the anticompetitive conduct by Microsoft. The Department does not have a view as to whether the space on the desktop should be viewed as the property of Microsoft or the computer manufacturers. The Department does have the view that Microsoft middleware and competing middleware should compete for the space, and the proposed Final Judgment ensures that this competition occurs.

Question 19. The CIS suggests the Department has embraced the goal of encouraging competitive development of "middleware" in order that such middleware can become the type of platform software that could challenge the operating system monopoly. The settlement requires Microsoft to allow OEMs to remove consumer "access" to the company's "middleware." It has been observed, however, that since the code for Microsoft's "middleware" is commingled with Windows, OEMs are only allowed to remove the icon for a middleware application. The CIS seems to acknowledge that Microsoft understood that software developers would only write to the APIs exposed by Navigator in numbers large enough to threaten the applications barrier to entry if they believe that Navigator would emerge as the standard software employed to browse the web. Can you explain why you believe third-party application developers would write applications to non-Microsoft APIs if the Microsoft middleware APIs as well as the Windows APIs will be present on over 95% of the personal computers sold?

Answer. The proposed Final Judgment will require Microsoft to do more than simply allow for the removal of its middleware icons. It requires that Microsoft allow end users and computer manufacturers to remove other means of access to, and override automatic invocations of, Microsoft middleware products and replace them with independently developed middleware products. Therefore, regardless of whether some portion of the Microsoft middleware code remains, end users and computer manufacturers can remove access to such middleware and replace it with alternative middleware. As the trial demonstrated, actual usage of a middleware product by the consumer, and not simply the presence of the product's code on the computer, has competitive significance. The marketplace, however, will determine whether any particular middleware product becomes sufficiently ubiquitous. This will ensure that competing middleware products will have the opportunity to compete for placement on the personal computer and that consumers will have a choice.

Question 20. Concerns have been raised about the consequences of several "provisos" that have been included in the PFJ. For example, Section III. H.3 prohibits Microsoft from denying consumers the choice of using competing applications, but a proviso to this language states that Microsoft can challenge a consumer's decision to choose an application other than its own after 14 days and encourage the consumer to switch back to the Microsoft product. What does the Department believe will be the impact of the messages that Microsoft will be able to send to consumers on their own computers? Are other companies permitted to send comparable messages to consumers who choose to utilize Microsoft products? Finally, why did the Department choose a period of 14 days as opposed to some other period of time?

Answer. It is incorrect that the proposed Final Judgment allows Microsoft to "challenge" a consumer's decision to select a non-Microsoft middleware product. Some end users prefer to have icons readily available on the desktop; others prefer a "clean desktop." In Windows XP, Microsoft has a Clean Desktop Wizard, which asks a user whether he or she would like to have unused icons (whether for Microsoft products or other products) taken off the desktop and placed in a folder, where they can still be easily accessed. The proposed Final Judgment allows Microsoft to continue providing this cleanup function, which the user can choose to take advantage of or not. The impact will be that end users can exercise choice. The proposed Final Judgment requires Microsoft to wait 14 days before it seeks confirmation from the end user because this will ensure that end users have a meaningful opportunity to determine which products, if any, they want to keep on the desktop.

Question 21. Under Sections III.H and VLN, a competing middleware application receives protection under the PFJ, but this protection applies only if the competitor ships at least one million units over the course of a year. Why did the Department choose that particular number? Did the Department give consideration to the argument that small innovators, who may be in the initial stages of product development and sales, might be in need of greater protection than a company capable of selling more than one million units?

Answer. The one million copies figure is implicated only in the operative provision contained in Section III.H. of the proposed Final Judgment and only to a very limited extent in Section III.D. Section III.H. requires N4icrosoft to include in Windows an effective add/remove function to allow end users and computer manufacturers to enable or remove access to Microsoft and non-Microsoft middleware products, and to permit non-Microsoft middleware products to take on a default status that will override middleware functions Microsoft has integrated into the operating system. Distribution of only one million copies, rather than sales, installation or usage, is a relatively minor threshold in the software industry today, and including this limited qualification in Section III.H. will ensure that Microsoft's affirmative obligations under these provisions will not be triggered by minor, or even nonexistent, products that have not established a competitive potential in the market and that might even be unknown to Microsoft development personnel. The one million copies figure applies in even a more limited fashion to Section III.D. That section requires Microsoft to disclose to software and hardware developers, computer manufacturers and others in the industry certain APIs and other technical information that Microsoft's middleware products use to interoperate with the Windows operating system. The one million copy limitation applies only to disclosures of interfaces for future middleware that has not yet been developed or even conceived. The Department considered the competitive impact of smaller innovators. In fact, the proposed Final Judgment provides protection for nascent middleware products by prohibiting Microsoft from retaliating or discriminating against them, regardless of the number of copies that they distribute.

Question 22.[The letter skips this question.]

Question 23. Section 111.13 of the PH prohibits Microsoft from engaging in discriminatory pricing of its desktop operating system with OEMs. Does the PH also prohibit use of this same kind of discriminatory pricing against server operating systems and other non-Windows software?

Answer. The proposed Final Judgment does not require Microsoft to use uniform terms and conditions when licensing its server operating system or other non-Windows software.

Question 24. The interim decree proposed by Judge Jackson included a provision precluding Microsoft from taking knowing action to disable or adversely affect the operation of competing middleware software. Does the PFJ contain a comparable provision? If not, what was the Department's rationale for not including this prohibition in the proposed settlement?

Answer. The proposed Final Judgment does not contain an express provision precluding Microsoft from taking knowing action to disable or adversely affect the operation of competing middleware products. As explained more fully in response to question 16, the Department chose not to include this type of provision because it would have given Microsoft a license to interfere with competing middleware as long as it simply notified the competing developer. In addition, it would have been difficult for the Department to enforce the provision because of the constant changes Microsoft makes to its operating system. Many of these changes would have been known by Microsoft to have the unintended consequence of affecting a competing product's interoperability. Instead, the proposed Final Judgment contains provisions that require Microsoft to provide competing middleware with APIs needed to interoperate with the Windows operating system.

Question 25. Why did the Department choose not to present evidence to the District Court on current PC operating system market developments, including changes in the Internet browser market share since the trial began? Did the Department undertake an investigation of current market developments to determine the impact of the PFJ on the existing market realities? For example, was there an analysis of the impact of the proposed settlement on Microsoft's proposed future products and services?

Answer. Judge Kollar-Kotelly had scheduled an evidentiary hearing on remedy to take place in 2002. The Department would have had the opportunity to present evidence to the Court at that time. There was no opportunity to present evidence to the Court at air earlier date. .

The Department conducted an ongoing evaluation of market developments and the impact of the proposed Final Judgment on existing market realities. One result of this evaluation was to broaden the definition of middleware to include new potential threats to the operating system, including e-mail clients, media players, instant messaging software and future middleware developments. The Department also analyzed the impact of the Court of Appeals' decision and the proposed Final Judgment on Microsoft's future products and services.

Question 26. The CIS suggests that the District Court's role under the Antitrust Procedures and Penalties Act is limited to reviewing the remedy in relationship to the violations that the United States has alleged in its complaint. *See* CIS at p. 67. Yet the authorities cited for that proposition appear to be cases that were settled before trial. Some observers argue that in this case the District Court should review the settlement in relationship to the Court of Appeals ruling rather than to the violations alleged in the original complaint. Does the Department agree with that assessment?

Answer. Beyond the Department's position set forth in its submissions to the Court, the Department cannot comment on the appropriate review by the Court because the Court's review of the proposed Final Judgment is pending under the Tunney Act.

Question 27. Has the Department undertaken any studies to determine the effectiveness of its prior consent decree with Microsoft in restoring competition? How do you believe prior obstacles to enforcement of consent decrees with Microsoft are addressed in the PFJ?

Answer. The Department has not conducted a formal study on the effectiveness of the prior consent decree with Microsoft. In its ongoing evaluation of the effectiveness of the proposed Final Judgment, however, the Department did consider the prior consent decree with Microsoft. There has been no determination by a court of obstacles to enforcement of consent decrees with Microsoft. Moreover, the proposed Final Judgment in this case contains some of the most stringent enforcement provisions contained in a modern consent decree. In addition to the ordinary prosecutorial access powers, the proposed Final Judgment requires an independent, full-time, on-site technical compliance team and a provision under which the term of the judgment may be extended by up to two years in the event the Court finds serious, systemic violations.

Question 28. Do you believe that current antitrust law is sufficient to guarantee not only competition but timely enforcement in areas such as the software industry?

Answer. The Department believes that the current antitrust laws are sufficient to guarantee not only competition, but timely enforcement in high-tech areas, such as the software industry.

Question 29. What steps, if any, should be taken, legislatively or otherwise, to ensure that the Department has the proper economic and technological resources to enforce the law in the software industry?

Answer. The Department does not believe that any changes to the antitrust laws are needed to ensure that the Department has the proper economic and technological resources to enforce the law in the software industry or other high-tech areas. The Department should continue to have the adequate resources to enforce the laws as long as appropriately funded by the Congress.

* * * *

Please do not hesitate to contact us if we can be of assistance on this or any other matter.

Responses of Jay L. Himes to Questions from by Senator Leahy

Question 1. A number of states are still litigating this case against Microsoft, and have submitted a remedy proposal to the district court. That proposal is stronger in significant respects than your proposed settlement. For example, they propose a court-appointed special master with the authority to gather evidence and conduct hearings as part of the enforcement mechanism.

(a) Do you believe that the more stringent provisions sought by the litigating states are not in the public interest?

(b) Did you consider restrictions similar to those sought by the non-settling parties or did you think that Microsoft would not agree to them?

Answer. (a) Estimating the impact on the public interest of one set of provisions said to be "more stringent" than another set of provisions, and reducing that impact by the costs associated with trying to achieve the "more stringent" provisions, is not readily accomplished, and such a process may be fairly susceptible to differences of opinion.

The Litigating States have proposed a final judgment (the "LSPFJ") in continuing litigation to which New York, among others, is a party, and in which New York may be called on to express positions relating to the remedy sought. Therefore, I do not believe it appropriate to comment on specific provisions in the LSPFJ.

(b) In participating in negotiations that led to the Revised Proposed Final Judgment, dated November 6, 2001 (the "PFJ"), I acted on behalf of all the plaintiff states (including the District of Columbia) in the cases brought against Microsoft. Rules of law constrain me, as a representative of only one of the plaintiffs in the Microsoft cases, from disclosing the contents of communications among the plaintiffs regarding particular remedial provisions considered during the negotiations period that led to the PFJ. However, in the negotiations between the plaintiffs and Microsoft during this period, some of the provisions included in the LSPFJ (or similar provisions) were put forth but not acceptable to Microsoft, or were put forth but withdrawn as part of the negotiating process that culminated in the PFJ.

Question 2. The Court of Appeals found that Microsoft's deception of Java developers and "pollution of the Java standard" constituted exclusionary practices in violation of Section 2 of the Sherman Act, and eliminated its competitive presence in the desktop realm. Unlike Navigator, Java may still be a viable competitive force, in other arenas. What provision, if any, in the settlement agreement prohibits Microsoft from repeating such an act?

Answer. The Court of Appeals' decision held that Microsoft violated section 2 of the Sherman Act by providing Java developers with tools that resulted in the developers writing programs that ran on the version of Java developed by Microsoft, but not on the version of Java developed by Sun, and that Microsoft knowingly failed to disclose this fact to the Java developers. *United States v. Microsoft*, 253 F.3d 34, 76–77 (D.C. Cir. 2001). If Microsoft engaged in comparable conduct with respect to software that competes with Microsoft Platform Software, or with any software that runs on any software that competes with Microsoft Platform Software, § III–F of the PFJ is likely to reach such conduct. "Retaliation" prohibited by § III–F properly includes the scenario in which: (a) a person referred to in § III–F is (for example) developing software that is intended to work with an operating system that competes with Windows, or that is a middleware product; and (b) Microsoft, knowing that, provides that person with tools that Microsoft knows will result in software that is compatible with Windows, but not compatible with the competing operating system or middleware product under development.

Question 3. As I understand the proposed settlement, Microsoft need only disclose APIs and documentation to middleware developers when Microsoft itself has a competing product. Some critics say this would allow Microsoft to determine the pace of innovation on the desktop by simply deciding not to develop or market competing products until it is ready with its own product—or until it has swallowed up a likely competitor. Allowing Microsoft, in essence, to determine the pace of desktop innovation would not aid the software industry generally, and not benefit consumers. How do you respond to this criticism?

Answer. The premise underlying this question is incorrect. In many circumstances—indeed, perhaps the large majority of the probable circumstances—Microsoft's obligations to disclose and document APIs under § III–D arise *whether or not* there exists in the marketplace a middleware product that competes with one released or developed by Microsoft itself. Further, in those circumstances where Microsoft might not have an obligation to document and disclose APIs, business constraints on Microsoft should make the risk that it might use nondisclosure to attempt to determine the pace of invocation more theoretical than real.

First, "Microsoft Middleware"—the triggering term for purposes of API disclosure and documentation—currently includes (by virtue of the definitional reference to "Microsoft Middleware Product") "the functionality provided by Internet Explorer, Microsoft's Java Virtual Machine, Windows Media Player, Windows Messenger, Outlook Express and their successors in the Windows Operating System Product [collectively, "§ VI–K(1) Middleware"]." (PFJ § VI–L, K; emphasis added) These are the most important types of middleware in existence today, and API disclosure and documentation is required whether or not another company has developed a competing product.

Second, the "successor" element of the part of the Microsoft Middleware Product definition quoted above should assure API disclosure and documentation for middleware subsequently developed by Microsoft whenever that subsequently developed middleware uses a more than insubstantial part of any of the § VI–K(1) Middleware in existence today. Again, another company need not market a competing product in order to trigger Microsoft's disclosure obligations.

If the "successor" element of the Microsoft Middleware Product definition does not apply, then the circumstance envisioned by this question could, in theory, arise. However, the likelihood of this circumstance resulting in Microsoft determining the pace of innovation at the PC level does not seem substantial.

As one scenario implicitly posited by this question: (a) Microsoft might contemplate a new, presumably significant, middleware product for which there is no comparable product in the 'marketplace; and (b) Microsoft refrains from developing the product, or from releasing it after its development because, by hypothesis, Microsoft seeks to determine the pace of industry innovation. This scenario seems unlikely because it assumes that Microsoft would voluntarily chose to forego the very "first mover" advantages that companies in the software industry typically seek to capture. The intangible benefits that could arise from trying to control the pace of innovation would not seem sufficiently great to warrant giving up the opportunity to be the first to introduce a significant new product, while taking the risk that another company will be able to seize the first mover advantages even without API disclosure and documentation.

Netscape, after all, introduced its Navigator browser before Microsoft offered one and achieved a significant usage share by virtue of being first in the marketplace. Thereafter, Microsoft attacked Navigator's success by the various anti-competitive conduct at the heart of the DOJ and States' cases. The notion that Microsoft would risk this very situation all over again by choosing to forego introducing a significant new middleware product seems remote. Furthermore, it is not clear how a judicial decree could address this particular scenario. It simply would not be practicable to order that Microsoft must develop new middleware products and then disclose and document their APIs so that others in the marketplace could develop competing products.

A second alternative scenario implicitly posited by this question—one where there is a new and significant middleware product in the marketplace—seems even less probable. On this second scenario, the business risks that Microsoft would face if it refrained from developing or releasing a competing product would be even greater than in the first scenario. Microsoft would, indeed, be giving up the first mover advantages to another company in an effort to thwart the pace of innovation by not making the API disclosure and documentation that could benefit the marketplace product. Meanwhile, the developer of the marketplace product would have the opportunity to devise the means to enable its product either to work well enough on Windows to make the product successful in the market, or to make the product work on another piece of software that already works well on Windows. (Again, that was what Netscape did when it introduced its browser.) So, Microsoft would plainly act at its business peril if it chose such a course of action.

Question 4. A loophole seems to be created by the exception to the requirement of APIs and documentation disclosure. Microsoft is supposed to disclose APIs, documentation, and communications protocols to permit interoperability of middleware and servers with Windows operating systems. But Microsoft does not need to disclose such information if it would, in *Microsoft's opinion*, compromise the security of various systems, which are very broadly defined. What do you say to the critics who fear that this loophole may swallow the API disclosure requirement?

Answer. I believe this is a misconception. The provision to which this question relates is PFJ § 111J(1), which applies, to begin with, *only* to enumerated categories of software: "anti-piracy, antivirus, software licensing, digital rights management, encryption or authentication systems." Further, for these enumerated categories of software, the exception from disclosure itself covers *only* "portions of APIs or Documentation or portions or layers of Communications Protocols the disclosure of which would compromise the security of a *particular installation or group of installations*" of this software. This narrow exception is limited to specific end-user implementations of security items, commonly referred to by such terms as "keys, authorization tokens or enforcement criteria." The disclosure exception embodied by § III–J(1) is not only very narrow, but also essential to preserving the security of the software systems involved.

Question 5. The non-settling states' proposed remedy requires Microsoft to release technical information necessary for middleware to be able to interoperate with Windows as soon as Microsoft gives its own developers that information. The proposed settlement only requires such disclosure when Microsoft puts out a major test version of a new Windows release. Presumably promotion of competition is the animating idea behind this provision, so why did you not insist that other non Microsoft developers have this information at the same time Microsoft developers did?

Answer. This timing provision, part of § III–D, is intended to ensure that non-Microsoft developers and others have disclosure in advance of the actual commercial releases of the relevant Microsoft software so that these third parties can make sure that their own competing products function on and interoperate with Windows. If disclosure is made too early in the product development process, non-Microsoft software developers may devote time and resources to writing potentially compatible software, while Microsoft may, as part of its normal product development process, change the software under development in ways that could have the effect of mooting all or part of the efforts of the non-Microsoft developer. The timing of disclosure takes these considerations into account.

Question 6. In 1995 the Department of Justice and Microsoft entered into a Consent Decree. Two years later the Department sued Microsoft for contempt of the Decree when Microsoft and the Department disagreed over the meaning and correct interpretation of certain provisions of the Decree, including the meaning of the word "integrate" as that term was used in the Decree. Given the prior litigation between the Department and Microsoft over the proper interpretation of the 1995 Consent Decree, do you agree that Microsoft and the settling plaintiffs should have a common, explicitunderstanding of the meaning and scope of this proposed Final Judgment before it is entered?

Answer. Parties should have a common understanding of the meaning and scope of the terms of an agreement, including a consent decree and in particular the PFJ, as of the time that they accept the terms of that agreement.

Question 7. Do you agree that the meaning and scope of the proposed Final Judgment as agreed upon by the settling plaintiffs and Microsoft should be precise, unambiguous and fully articulated so that the public at large can understand and rely on your mutual understanding of the Judgment?

Answer. I consider it most important that the terms of the PFJ be sufficiently clear that persons conversant in the business and its terminology—as opposed to the public at large—can understand the PFJ, and govern their affairs accordingly. I believe that the PFJ accomplishes this goal.

Question 8. If Microsoft were to disagree with the settling plaintiffs' interpretation of one or more important provisions of the proposed Final Judgment, would you consider that to be a potentially seriousproblem?

Answer. If Microsoft were to disagree with the settling plaintiffs' "interpretation" (which I take to be synonymous with "understanding") of one or more important provisions of the PFJ, that could be a potentially serious problem, depending on such matters as: (a) the degree of disagreement; (b) whether the disagreement promoted or retarded the purposes of the provision involved; (c) whether Microsoft's understanding retarded the purposes of the provision involved; (d) whether Microsoft intended to conform its conduct only to its own understanding of the provision; (e) whether the disagreement was soluble under the provisions governing the activities of the Technical Committee under the PFJ or under any other part of PFJ; and (f) the practical or foreseeable effect of the disagreement, if not resolved, in the real world.

Question 9. Do you agree that it would be highly desirable to identify any significant disagreement between Microsoft and the settling plaintiffs over the correct interpretation of the proposed Final Judgment now, before the Judgment is entered by the Court, rather than through protracted litigation as in the case of the 1995 Consent Decree?

Answer. If there were a disagreement over the terms of the PFJ between Microsoft and the settling plaintiffs—and if that disagreement could be termed "significant," after taking into account sorts of considerations referred to in response to question 8—it would be desirable to identify that disagreement.

Question 10. Does the Competitive Impact Statement set forth the settling plaintiffs' definitive interpretation of its proposed Final Judgment with Microsoft?

Answer. The Competitive Impact Statement ("CIS") is a document that the United States Department of Justice prepared and filed pursuant to 15 U.S.C. §§ 16(b)–(h). Although the document was not filed on behalf of New York, I am not aware of any views expressed by DOJ in the CIS that differ in a material respect from mine. I would not, however, characterize the CIS as a "definitive interpretation" of the PFJ, both because I do not understand what that expression refers to in this context, and because, in any event, the PFJ necessarily is best understood (or "interpreted") and applied with reference to a specific fact setting, involving specific conduct.

Question 11. Has Microsoft informed the settling plaintiffs that it has any disagreement with the interpretation of the Final Judgment as set forth in the Competitive Impact Statement?

Answer. As suggested above in response to Question 10, I am uncertain whether the CIS is appropriately described as an "interpretation" of the PFJ. However, Microsoft has not expressed to me any disagreement with the contents of the CIS; nor have I been told that Microsoft has expressed any such disagreement to any other settling plaintiff.

Question 12. Can the public at large rely upon the Competitive Impact Statement as the definitive interpretation of the nature and scope of Microsoft's obligations under the Final Judgment?

Answer. The CIS is a document required to be filed by DOJ. For the reasons noted in response to question 10, I would not refer to the CIS as "the definitive interpretation of the nature and scope of Microsoft's obligations" under the PFJ.

Question 13. If the public cannot rely on the interpretation of the proposed Final Judgment as set forth in the Competitive Impact Statement, then what is the mutually understood and agreed-upon interpretation of the meaning and scope of Microsoft's obligations under the Final Judgment?

Answer. Microsoft's obligations under the settlement are set forth in the PFJ, the terms of which are to be interpreted in accordance with their general meaning in the industry. In addition, the parties that negotiated the settlement believe that there is a "mutual understanding" of the meaning and scope of the terms of the PFJ. Moreover, although the CIS is not a "definitive interpretation" of the settlement, as noted above, to my knowledge Microsoft has not indicated to any settling plaintiff any disagreement with the terms of that document.

Responses of Jay L. Himes to questions from Senator Hatch

Question 1. I realize that you support the Proposed Settlement on the basis that it compares favorably to the set of remedies that many predict have resulted from further litigation. However, setting that aside for the moment, could you tell us what particular merit—if any—you see in the Remedial Proposals filed by the non-settling states?

Answer. The Litigating States have proposed the LSPFJ in continuing litigation to which New York, among others, is a party, and in which New York may be called on to express positions relating to the remedy sought. Therefore, I do not believe it appropriate to comment on specific provisions in the LSPFJ or on the LSPFJ generally.

Question 2. Please expand specifically on the pros and cons of the various proposals for alternative enforcement mechanisms that were considered and rejected in the settlement discussions. In particular could you give us your view of the provision, contained in the non-settling parties' Remedial Proposal, that would provide for a special master?

Answer. The enforcement section of the PFJ (§ IV) includes: (a) relatively common "visitation" provisions empowering the DOJ and State enforcers to undertake enforcement activity (§ IV–A); (b) the establishment of an internal compliance officer at Microsoft with specified powers and responsibilities (§ IV–C and parts of § IV–D)—also a relatively common type of provision; and (c) the creation of what is referred to in the PFJ as the "Technical Committee" or "TC," which is charged with the responsibility to assist the governments' enforcement activity. (§ IV–B and parts of § IV–D) In my written testimony, I said that the PFJ contains "an enforcement mechanism that we believe is unprecedented in any antitrust case," and that is "probably the strongest ever crafted in an antitrust case." (Testimony of Jay L. Himes, dated December 12, 2001, pp. 12, 14) In expressing that view, I had in mind the enforcement provisions in general, and particularly the addition of TC to the more common enforcement provisions found in the PFJ. Since the PFJ was announced in early November 2001, no one has called to my attention any antitrust case where a court adopted an enforcement mechanism comparable in strength to the one that DOJ and the Settling States negotiated.

Most of the negotiations concerning the enforcement section related to what became the TC provisions. Therefore, I will focus my remarks on this aspect of the PFJ, bearing in mind that the TC is only part of the total enforcement mechanism.

From my point of view (and I reiterate that I am speaking here only on behalf of New York), the central elements of this part of the enforcement mechanism, which I sought to achieve, were the following:

(a) the creation of a body outside of the government enforcers, which would augment the resources of, and would have as its mission assisting, DOJ and the States in enforcement,

(b) the on-site presence of this body at Microsoft;

(c) the conferral of expansive powers on this body to assist the enforcement effort; and

(d) the payment of this enforcement effort by Microsoft, together with provisions designed to discourage Microsoft from challenging expenses incurred.

A review of the § IV of PFJ shows that, despite the need for negotiations with Microsoft, we secured each of the four central elements that I have described. The TC will be composed of persons with software expertise, who will have extensive, on-site authority to assist in enforcement of and compliance with the PFJ, and who will be independent of Microsoft.

The negotiations also resulted in adding provisions to the TC mechanism. For example:

1. The TC has a voluntary dispute resolution function, which could be thought of as going beyond typical law enforcement activity. (PFJ § IV–D) This function is designed to facilitate resolving issues that may arise under the PFJ in an expeditious fashion. The basic object here is to help assure that the PFJ achieves the marketplace effects that it is intended to achieve.

2. The PFJ directs that "[n]o work product, findings or recommendations of the TC may be admitted in any enforcement proceeding before the Court," and that "no member of the TC shall testify" in any proceeding regarding any matter relating to the PFJ. (PFJ § IV–D(4)(d)) These provisions are designed, in part, to reduce the need that Microsoft might otherwise feel to call on its attorneys immediately to become involved whenever the TC makes a request to speak with Microsoft employees, or to obtain documents or other information. These provisions are also designed to recognize that the extensive access to information afforded to the TC under the PFJ should be used only to further the TC's enforcement and dispute resolution functions, and not to assist non-parties in other cases brought against Microsoft.

In my written testimony to the Committee, I noted that the limitation on admission of TC material into evidence should not have a great impact. (Testimony of Jay L. Himes, dated December 12, 2001, p. 14) That is so because government enforcement officials still will be able to use the TC's work. Moreover, § IV(A)(2) of the PFJ gives DOJ and the Settling States independent access to Microsoft documents (including source code), and employees. That authority, together with the TC's work, should enable the government enforcers, working with their experts, promptly to evaluate and replicate the TC's work for use in judicial proceedings.

Beyond this, I am constrained to reiterate that the Litigating States have proposed the LSPFJ in continuing litigation to which New York, among others, is a party, and in which New York may be called on to express positions relating to the remedy sought. Therefore, I do not believe it appropriate to comment on the special master provisions in the LSPFJ.

Question 3. Please explain, from the perspectives of the settling State plaintiffs, whether and how the Proposed Settlement sufficiently protects against Microsoft leveraging its monopoly power in operating systems into the Internet-based services market and the server market?

Answer. The "server/client interop" provision of the PFJ—§ III–E—will prevent Microsoft from incorporating into Windows features or functionality with which its own server software can interoperate, and then refusing to make available information about those features or functions that non-Microsoft servers need in order to have the same opportunities to interoperate with Windows. Thus, § III–E is designed to prevent Microsoft from using its Windows monopoly to gain advantages in the communications line between PCs and servers, which are not available to non-Microsoft servers. This is accomplished by mandating disclosure of Communications Protocols. The ultimate objective is to encourage developers to write middleware operating at the server level, which can provide functionality to PCs, and which may, in turn, erode the applications barrier to entry that protects Microsoft's Windows operating system monopoly at the PC level.

The district court dismissed the States' monopoly leveraging claim in its 1998 summary judgment ruling, and that ruling was not the subject of the appeal to the D.C. Circuit from the final judgment entered in June 2000. Accordingly, the possible "leveraging" of Microsoft's monopoly power in PC operating systems into "the Internet-based services market and the server market" involves matters that are not readily regarded as within either the scope of liability established by the D.C. Circuit or within the appropriate remedy in the case remanded by the Court of Appeals.

Responses of Jay L. Himes to questions from Senator DeWine

Question 1. The term of the proposed settlement is only five years, while many other antitrust consent decrees last for ten years. It has been suggested that a shorter time period is justified because this industry changes rapidly and a longer decree may not be warranted after five years. Given that the Department of Justice has the ability to go to the court and seek to modify a consent decree or terminate it if market conditions warrant such a change, why not impose a longer period of enforcement, and then decide later if it needs to be modified or abandoned?

Answer. The term of the decree is appropriate in light of the rapidly changing character of the industry and the facts of this particular case. The alternative described in this question—a longer decree that could, on application to the court, be shortened based on market conditions—is not a common approach.

Question 2. As the Court of Appeals in this case noted, the Supreme Court has indicated that a remedies decree in an antitrust case must seek to "unfetter a market from anticompetitive conduct," "terminate the illegal monopoly, deny to the defendant the fruits of its statutory violation, and ensure that there remain no practices likely to result in monopolization in the future." Do you believe that this is the appropriate standard to use? If so, does the proposed final judgment deny Microsoft the fruits of its illegal acts? Specifically, can you discuss whether Microsoft has been denied the fruits of its effort to maintain a monopoly in the operating system?

Answer. The PFJ has been submitted in a continuing litigation in which New York may be required to take positions. Therefore, I do not believe it appropriate to comment on issues of law that may arise in this ongoing litigation.

As to the second part of this question, I regard the "fruits" of Microsoft's monopoly maintenance activity to be the fortification of the applications barrier to entry that protects Microsoft's Windows monopoly at the PC level. Through a variety of different means—including conduct prohibitions, Windows pricing obligations, and affirmative design and disclosures obligations—the PFJ seeks to deny that fortification to Microsoft.

Question 3. The proposed settlement has some prohibitions against Microsoft retaliating against computer manufacturers that place competing software on their computers—these provisions are intended to allow manufacturers to offer non-Microsoft products if they choose. I understand that Microsoft currently offers incentives to computer manufacturers if they can get computers to "boot up" quickly. Some believe that computer manufacturers will not want to slow down the start-up time by placing additional software on the computer because they will risk losing the incentive payment. Does the proposed settlement deal with this problem.

Answer. Based on my understanding, this should not be a meaningful problem. The types of middleware likely to be installed by OEMs should not have a material effect on the speed of the boot sequence. If Microsoft were to condition incentives on boot up standards that were so onerous as to discourage OEMs from installing competing middleware, that would suggest that the express purpose of the program is pretextual. Microsoft's conduct would constitute prohibited retaliation under § III–A.

Question 4. The Appellate Court noted that the applications barrier protects Microsoft's operating system monopoly. The Court stated that this allows Microsoft the ability to maintain its monopoly even in the face of competition from potentially "superior" new rivals. In what manner do you believe the proposed settlement addresses the applications barrier?

Answer. Please see the second paragraph of my response to question 2 from Senator DeWine.

Question 5. Some believe that unless Microsoft is prevented from commingling operating system code with middleware code, competitors will not be able to truly compete in the middleware market. Because the code is commingled, the Microsoft products cannot be removed even if consumers don't want them. This potentially deters competition in at least two respects. First, as the Appellate Court found, commingling deters computer manufacturers from pre-installing rival software. And second, it seems that software developers are more likely to write their programs to operate on Microsoft's middleware if they know that the Microsoft middleware will always be on the computer whereas competing products may not be. Even if consumers are unaware that code is commingled, shouldn't we be concerned about the market impact of commingling code? What is the upside of allowing it to be commingled, and on the other hand, what concerns are raised by removing the code?

Answer. I do not read the D.C. Circuit's decision as finding that commingling of code, standing alone, deters OEMs from pre-installing rival software. I also doubt that commingling code in the Windows operating system is, in itself, of competitive significance vis-a-vis the consumer. Rather, as the liability trial demonstrated, the consumer's actual usage of middleware—not simply the presence of the product's software code on the computer—has competitive significance. Thus, so far as I am aware, throughout this case both DOJ and the States did not argue that there was a need for Microsoft (or OEMs) to remove Windows software code in order to give choice to consumers. Accordingly, removing the visible means of end-user access to Microsoft middleware as a means of customizing the operating system, while not requiring that software code itself be removed, remediates the concerns expressed.

As to the benefits and costs of removing code, I reiterate that the Litigating States have proposed the LSPFJ in continuing litigation to which New York, among others, is a party, and in which New York may be called on to express positions relating to the remedy sought. Therefore, I do not believe it appropriate to comment on specific provisions in the LSPFJ.

I will, nevertheless, offer my own personal views generally on the subject of whether or not to remove software code.

The principal benefit from non-removal of Windows code is that the code remains available if an enduser prefers to use the Microsoft product, instead of using the competing middleware installed by an OEM. That end-user may then choose to "undo" the OEM's installation decision with a minimum of effort. At the same time, I am not persuaded that there is a significant upside to requiring software code to be removed. As noted above, the presence or absence of software code on a PC probably is not, standing alone, competitively significant. Further, computer hardware capability is, today, sufficiently great that removing code is not likely to improve PC performance insignificant respects. Also, even if code were removed it could be readily restored via downloading the code over the Internet, as well as by reinstalling it using a CD. The ease with which a download can be accomplished is likely to increase over time.

On the other hand, there are costs to removing code. Removal would require an engineering effort to identify specific places where the Windows operating system can be said to end, and middleware (or conceivably other applications) can be said to begin. The remaining operating system, and the code removed, would then need to be subjected to a battery of tests to make sure that both performed the way that they were intended to perform, and in fact previously performed, absent the removal. That could be a formidable task, depending on (among other things) the significance of the code removed and the number and type of non-Microsoft applications written to it. Moreover, any effort to remove code could implicate the court in reviewing difficult issues of software engineering, design and performance.

Question 6. Many believe that this settlement proposal merely requires Microsoft to stop engaging in illegal conduct, but does little in the way of denying Microsoft the benefits of its bad acts. First, how would you answer these critics? Is this just a built-in reality of civil antitrust remedies, *i.e.*, that they don't aim to punish? And second, do you believe the remedy here is strong enough to dissuade other potential monopolists from engaging in the type of conduct in which Microsoft engaged?

Answer. My written testimony describes the various ways in which I believe the PFJ will promote competition in the computer and computer software industries. As noted above, I also believe that the PFJ denies Microsoft the fortification of the applications barrier to entry that Microsoft sought, by its anticompetitive conduct, to erect. I therefore believe that the PFJ offers a strong, effective remedy to the conduct that the Court of Appeals found to be unlawful. I similarly believe that the PFJ will have the effect of deterring other potential antitrust violators.

Question 7. Nine states didn't join with the Department of Justice's proposed final judgment because they didn't believe it adequately addressed competitive problems. These states recently filed their own remedy proposals. These states assert that one fruit of Microsoft's illegal conduct is Microsoft's dominant share of the internet browser market. They propose to deny Microsoft this benefit of its violations by requiring it to open-source the code for Internet Explorer. What do you believe the competitive impact of such action would be?

Answer. The Litigating States have proposed the LSPFJ in continuing litigation to which New York, among others, is a party, and in which New York may be called on to express positions relating to the remedy sought. Therefore, I do not believe it appropriate to comment on specific provisions in the LSPFJ.

Question 8. Given Microsoft's monopoly power in the operating system, some believe that merely allowing computer manufacturers to place competing software and icons on the operating system will not impede Microsoft's ability to capture a dominant share of any product that it binds to its operating system. Do you believe that media players, instant messaging services, and other companies products will be able to compete with similar MS products that are bound to the operating system?

Answer. Yes. I believe that the PFJ will give developers of competing middleware the information needed to enable them to design software that works well with Windows, and that other parts of the PFJ will empower OEMs to add competing middleware to Windows. Further, the PFJ includes extensive provisions that will enable competing middleware to be substituted into the operating system in lieu of Microsoft middleware.

Question 9. Many have criticized the proposed final judgment saying it has loopholes in it that will allow Microsoft to continue operating as it has done in the past. For example, the proposed final judgment clearly seeks to prevent Microsoft from retaliating against computer manufacturers that install competing software onto the computer. However, because the provisions are limited to specific practices or types of software, and apply only to "agreements" between Microsoft and computer manufacturers, many believe that Microsoft will find alternative methods of controlling the practices of computer manufacturers. Do you believe competition would be better served if Microsoft were broadly prohibited from retaliating against computer manufacturers?

Answer. I believe that the PFJ does broadly prohibit Microsoft from retaliating against OEMs. Section III–A, in pertinent part, provides that:

"Microsoft shall not retaliate against an OEM by altering Microsoft's commercial relations with that OEM, or by withholding newly introduced forms of non-monetary Consideration (including but not limited to new versions of existing forms of non-monetary Consideration) from that OEM, because it is known to Microsoft that the OEM is or is contemplating:

1. developing, distributing, promoting, using, selling, or licensing any software that competes with Microsoft Platform Software or any product or service that distributes or promotes any Non-Microsoft Middleware;

2. shipping a Personal Computer that (a) includes both a Windows Operating System Product and a non-Microsoft Operating System, or (b) will boot with more than one Operating System; or

3. exercising any of the options or alternatives provided for under this Final Judgment.

If an OEM seeks, for example, to add competing middleware to Windows, and Microsoft knows of that intention, any "alteration]" of Microsoft's "commercial relations" with that OEM—*regardless* of the means or products used to alter those commercial relations—implicates the non-retaliation protections of § III–A. So too would Microsoft's failure to offer that OEM "newly introduced forms of non-monetary Consideration." "Consideration," in this context, is itself broadly defined and embraces, in non-monetary form:

"provision of preferential licensing terms; technical, marketing, and sales support; enabling programs; product information; information about future plans; developer support; hardware or software certification or approval; or permission to display trademarks, icons or logos."

(PFJ § VIC)

If Microsoft were to engage in any such acts, there would be a presumption of wrongful retaliation against the OEM. The burden would be on Microsoft to justify its conduct under a limited exception provided for in the PFJ to permit pro-competitive activity.

It is important to note as well that, retaliation, for purposes of § III–A, is not limited to Microsoft's use of *any* particular software as a retaliation device. Instead, it is the change in any commercial relation between Microsoft and the OEM—however accomplished—that is important.

Also, insofar as the PFJ restricts certain "agreements" made by Microsoft (*see, e.g.*, PFJ §§ III–C(6), F(2), G), the term "agreement" is *not* defined, and, therefore, takes on its ordinary usage in the antitrust context. Thus, under the PFJ, the term "agreement" reaches *all* contracts, combinations, concerts of action or understandings—whether written or oral, and whether express or implied—that the antitrust laws ordinarily reach.

Question 10. The Court of Appeals ruled that Microsoft's practices which undermined the competitive threat of Sun's Java technology was an antitrust violation. The remedy proposed by the states that do not support the DOJ's proposed settlement would require Microsoft to distribute Java with its browser as a means of restoring Java's position in the market. Do you believe this would be beneficial to competition? What does the proposed final judgment do to restore this competition?

Answer. The PFJ should enable OEMs to add Java to Windows, free from the risk of retaliation from Microsoft, if the OEMs believe that there is consumer demand for that software.

The Litigating States have proposed the LSPFJ in continuing litigation to which New York, among others, is a party, and in which New York may be called on to express positions relating to the remedy sought. Therefore, I do not believe it appropriate to comment on specific provisions in the LSPFJ.

Question 11. Definition U. of the Proposed Final Judgment appears to allow Microsoft to determine in its sole discretion what constitutes the operating system. The Court of Appeals left open the possibility of a tying case against Microsoft. Will this provision essentially foreclose any opportunity of bringing a tying claim against Microsoft? Why do you give Microsoft the ability to make this determination?

Answer. Definition U defines the term "Windows Operating System Product" for purposes of the PFJ only. Nothing in the PFJ confers on Microsoft immunity from any antitrust liability that would otherwise arise in the absence of the decree. Therefore, Microsoft's conduct in adding software to Windows will remain subject to possible antitrust challenge on various grounds, one of which is unlawful tying.

In my personal view, giving Microsoft the ability to determine the contents of the Windows Operating System Product for purposes of the PFJ was consistent with the notion that OEMs could add competing middleware to Windows, and that removal of Windows software code by either Microsoft or OEMs was not required.

Parenthetically, let me emphasize that, under the PFJ, consequences to Microsoft can arise by virtue of its including software code in Windows. For example, code included in Windows can also meet the requirements of the Microsoft Middleware and Microsoft Middleware Product definitions. To that extent, code that is part of Windows can trigger the provisions of the PFJ obligating Microsoft to make API disclosure and to afford configuration options. Similarly, the "server/client interop provision"—§ III–E—requires Microsoft to disclose and license any Communications Protocols used by any part of Windows to interoperate natively with a Microsoft server. So, including code in Windows can trigger these Microsoft obligations as well.

Question 12. It has been indicated that one motivation for entering into this settlement was to provide immediate relief and avoid lengthy court proceedings. At the same time, many of the provisions of the settlement don't become active for up to 12 months after the settlement is enacted. Given your belief that relief should be immediate, why wait so long for these provisions to become active?

Answer. Under the PFJ, Microsoft is required to include in Windows an effective add/remove function to allow OEMS and end-users to enable or remove access to Microsoft and non-Microsoft middleware, as well as to permit non-Microsoft middleware to "override" (*i.e.*, become the default for) middleware functions that Microsoft has integrated into the operating system. Microsoft also is required to disclose and document the APIs between Windows and Microsoft middleware. Lead time is necessarily to enable Microsoft to make the changes to Windows that are needed to discharge its obligations under the PFJ.

The 12 month period that I believe is referred to in this question relates both to: (a) the "API disclosure provision"—§ III–D—which obligates Microsoft to disclose and document APIs between 'Microsoft Middleware and a Windows Operating System Product; and (b) the "operating system configuration" provision—§ III–H—which ensures that OEMs will be able to choose to offer and promote, and consumers be able to choose to use, Non-Microsoft Middleware Products. Microsoft needed time to identify all the APIs subject to § III–D, and to create the documents associated with disclosing these APIs. The period given to do this is "*the earlier* of the release of Service Pack 1 for Windows XP *or* 12 months after the submission" of the PFJ to the Court. (§ III–D; emphasis added) The first service pack for a new operating system is typically released within a few months. But recognizing the additional burdens on Microsoft arising from the PFJ, a 12 months maximum period was agreed to.

For a new version of the Windows Operating System Product, § III–D requires Microsoft to make disclosure "in a Timely Manner." This latter term is defined to refer to the time that "Microsoft first releases a beta test version of a Windows Operating System Product that is distributed to 150,000 or more beta testers." (PFJ § VI–R) As noted in my response to question 5 by Senator Leahy, this particular time period is based on a point in the product development process at which the software product design probably will be sufficiently far along as to enable independent software developers to devote the time and resources to writing potentially compatible software with limited risk that Microsoft product changes could moot such efforts.

Similarly, for a new Windows Operating System Product, § III–H obligates Microsoft to make the necessary operating system changes based on the "Microsoft Middleware Products which exist seven months prior to the last beta test version (i.e., the one immediately preceding the first release candidate) of that Windows Operating System Product." The purpose of this time period is to "freeze," as of a particular point in time, the group of Microsoft Middleware Products for which Microsoft must incorporate default settings into the Windows design. There has to be a specific point in time as of which Microsoft is permitted to identify the middleware for which it needs to make design accommodations, an assessment that itself needs to take into account the group of NonMicrosoft Middleware in the marketplace. (This is so because the term Microsoft Middleware Product depends, in certain circumstances, on the existence of a Non-Microsoft Middleware Product of similar functionality. PFJ § VI–K(2)(6)(ii).) It simply would not be realistic or fair to require Microsoft to base these design considerations on an ever-changing universe of non-Microsoft middleware.

Question 13. One provision of the proposed final judgment requires Microsoft to allow consumers or computer manufacturers to enable access to competing products. However, it appears that III.H. of the Stipulation and VI.N. indicate that for a product to qualify for these protections it must have a million copies distributed in the United States within the previous year. This seems to run contrary to the traditional antitrust philosophy of promoting new competition. Is this in fact the case? And if so, why are these protections limited to larger competitors?

Answer. The term Non-Microsoft Middleware Product is used (among other places) to identify software products that may be installed in lieu of a Microsoft Middleware Product, as provided in § III–H. One element of the definition of Non-Microsoft Middleware Product requires that one million copies be distributed in the United States within the previous year. This requirement refers only to copies distributed, not to copies sold, installed or used, and should not be difficult to meet, given the numerous distribution channels available today, including PC user-initiated download requests. This element is intended to strike a balance between triggering Microsoft's affirmative obligations—including the API disclosures required by § III–D and the creation of the mechanisms required by § III–H—and the competitive potential of minor products that have not established a meaningful presence in the market and that might even be unknown to Microsoft development personnel.

Response of Jay L. Himes to a question from Senator Kohl

Question. Mr. Himes, as you know, nine of your fellow states that originally joined you and the federal government in suing Microsoft have refused to consent to this settlement, and, just last Friday, proposed additional remedies. Why did these other states split ranks with you and the federal government? Would you be willing to consider modifications to this proposed settlement in order to gain their assent?

Answer. In participating in the negotiations that led to of the PFJ, I acted on behalf of all the plaintiff States (including the District of Columbia) in the cases brought against Microsoft. Rules of law constrain me, as a representative of only one of the plaintiffs in the Microsoft cases, from disclosing the contents of communications among the plaintiff States regarding possible courses of action, or the reasons for them, prior to the point that individual plaintiff States decided whether or not to accept the PFJ. Moreover, I do not believe it appropriate for me to speculate or offer my own interpretation of the reasons that nine plaintiff States decided not to accept the PFJ.

With respect to possible modifications of the PFJ, if the Litigating States and Microsoft jointly sought the involvement of New York in a process designed to modify the PFJ, we would of course participate in such an effort.

SUBMISSIONS FOR THE RECORD

Statement of Jonathan Zuck, President, Association for Competitive Technology, Washington, D.C.

INTRODUCTION

Good morning, Mr. Chairman and members of the Committee. I am Jonathan Zuck, President of the Association for Competitive Technology, or ACT. On behalf of our member companies, it is my sincere honor to testify before this Committee today. As a professional software developer and technology educator, I am grateful for this opportunity and appreciate greatly your interest in learning more about the effects of the proposed settlement entered into by the United States Department of Justice (DOJ), nine state attorneys general and Microsoft on our industry. ACT is a national, Information Technology (IT) industry group, founded by entrepreneurs and representing the full spectrum of technology firms. Our members include household names such as Microsoft, e-Bay and Orbitz. However, the vast majority of our members are small and midsize business, including software developers, IT trainers, technology consultants, dot-coms, integrators and hardware developers located in your states. The majority of ACT members cannot hire lawyers and lobbyists or fly to Washington to have their views heard. Therefore, they look to ACT to represent their interests. To be sure, to meet the needs of our broad constituency, we don't always agree with our members, even Microsoft, on some policy issues.

I have a great deal of respect and sympathy for the plight of these small technology companies, because I spent over fifteen years running similar companies. During this time, I've managed as many as 300 developers, taught over a hundred classes, and worked on some interesting projects. I was responsible for a loan evaluation application for Freddie Mac, an automated Fitness Report application for the Navy and a Regional Check Authentication system for the Department of Treasury. I have built software oil multiple platforms include DOS. DR–DOS, OS/2 and Windows using tools from many vendors including Microsoft, Oracle, Sybase, Powersoft,

IBM, Borland and others. I remain active as a technologist and last year designed a system to get to your corporate data wirelessly. I have also delivered keynotes and other presentations at technical conferences around the world.

While ACT members vary in their size and businesses, they share a common desire to maintain the competitive character of today's vibrant technology sector that has been responsible for America's "new economy." Unfortunately, for the last three years, the tens of thousands of small businesses in the IT industry have been virtually ignored during the government's investigation and prosecution of Microsoft.

I believe the settlement, on balance, is good not only for the bulk of the IT industry, but for consumers as well. Voters also see the value in the settlement. Voter Consumer Research conducted polls of 1,000 eligible voters last month in Utah and Kansas that are quite telling. In Utah and Kansas, when asked if their state attorney general should pursue the case after the DOJ settlement had been reached, the respondents said, *by a 6 to 1 margin*, that they should not.

As one of the "techies" on this panel, I look forward to getting into more "real life" effects of the proposed settlement to prove this point.

With that backdrop, my testimony today is focused on describing how the settlement will foster competition for thousands of America's small IT companies and how that, in turn, will benefit consumers.

THE STATE OF OUR INDUSTRY

Before we discuss life in a post Microsoft settlement world, I must speak to present-day competition and innovation. I want to begin by stating *unequivocally* that, counter to the protestations of some "experts," competition in the IT industry is alive and well. One demonstrable example is amount of capital investment by Venture Capitalists (VCs) and where that money is headed. Despite the recent downturn, VCs are still looking for the next "billion dollar deal." I know because I have worked with many of them. I won't get into the negative impact this "home-run or nothing" strategy has had on our industry but suffice it to say, billion dollar deals do not come from investing in mature markets with limited growth potential and large existing players. Billion dollar deals only come from investing in new markets with unlimited growth potential and those do not include office productivity software market or even the general PC software market. Indeed, a recent survey of VC's conducted by the DEMOletter, showed that nearly a third of those surveyed will invest over $100 million in start-ups in 2002 and that nearly 20 per cent are planning to invest up to $250 million.[1] The sectors of the IT industry receiving this money include software and digital media.[2] These are precisely the sectors that would benefit from this settlement. Suggestions that opposing the settlement would encourage VC's to change their stripes are ridiculous.

In fact, the information technology world is experiencing a shift away from desktop computing and toward other devices such as personal digital assistants (PDA's), cell phones, set top boxes/game consoles, web terminals and powerful servers that connect them all. In all these growth markets, competition is very strong even though Microsoft is present. As of the third quarter of this year, more than 52 percent of all PDA's were shipped with the Palm operating system while only 18 percent carried a Microsoft operating system according to Gartner. With cell phone manufacturers rushing to integrate PDA functionality, there is are several large players including Symbian (a joint venture between Nokia, Motorola, Ericsson, Matsushita [Panasonic], and Psion), Palm, Linux and Research in Motion's Blackberry operating system. In the game console/set-box arenas, Microsoft is just entering the picture with established companies like Sony and Nintendo standing on large installed user bases.

The server market is probably the best example of this growing competition. According to IDC, Linux's worldwide market share of new and upgraded operating systems for servers was 27 percent in 2000. It was second only to Microsoft, which stood at 42 percent. IDC predicts predicted Linux's market share will expand to 41 percent by 2005, while Microsoft's will only grow to 46 percent. Things should only become more competitive with IBM putting a billion dollars into its Linux push this year. The vigorous competition in this space proves in the absence of government intervention, companies like Linux can thrive.

BENEFITS OF THE SETTLEMENT

As the members of the Committee are doubtlessly aware, on November 2, 2001 the DOJ and Microsoft tentatively agreed on a settlement (or consent decree) de-

---

[1] DEMOletter, December 2001, at 5–6.
[2] Id., at 5.

signed to end the federal antitrust suit. Soon thereafter, nine states attorneys general signed off on a revised settlement. The proposed settlement succeeds in striking a difficult compromise between the "drastically altered" finding of liability adopted by the Court of Appeals and the wishes of Microsoft competitors and critics for crippling sanctions against the company.[3] Remarkably, the negotiators have worked out a settlement proposal that, while entirely satisfying to none, includes something for everyone.

A number of Microsoft competitors and their advocates have suggested that this agreement is flawed in that it "does not prevent Microsoft from leveraging its monopoly into other markets." This argument is based on an unfounded fear that Microsoft will attempt to monopolize other markets such as instant messaging and digital media. Undermining this argument is the fact that the Court of Appeals found unanimously that Microsoft did not use its monopoly in the browser (or middleware) market.[4] The bottom line is that the settlement was focused on addressing the allegedly anticompetitive conduct of the past and preventing similar conduct in the future. It is entirely consistent with the basic tenet of antitrust law, which is to protect consumers and competition, not competitors.

With that understanding, it is important to address the benefits the industry and consumer will derive from implementation of the proposed settlement. ACT believes that the benefits of the settlement can be classified as follows:

1. Increased flexibility for Original Equipment Manufacturers (OEMs)
2. Increased flexibility for third party IT companies
3. Greater consumer choice
4. Effective enforcement

I will discuss each benefit in turn, paying particular attention to the positive effects on competition in our industry.

1. Increased flexibility for Original Equipment Manufacturers (OEMs)

OEMs play a pivotal role in "supply chain" of delivering a rich computing experience for consumers. They provide independent software vendors (ISVs), many of whom are small IT companies, a valuable conduit by which to sell their wares directly to consumers by vying for space on the computer desktop. Thus, it is critical that OEMs have the flexibility to meet market demands by negotiating with ISVs for this type of placement. This practice is known as "monetizing the desktop" and is consistent with market-based competition. Under the proposed settlement, OEMs will have the flexibility to develop, distribute, use, sell, or license any software that competes with Windows or Microsoft "middleware[5]" without restrictions or any kind of retaliation from Microsoft.[6] Reinforcing this flexibility, the settlement prohibits Microsoft from even entering into agreements that obligate OEMs to any exclusive or fixed-percentage arrangements.[7] This allows OEMs to negotiate with an array of ISVs through the use of any number of incentives. Moreover, OEMs obtain some control over the desktop space for such things as icons and shortcuts.[8] Another critical element allowing the OEMs to create a competitive playing field is that they have the ability to have nonMicrosoft operating systems (e.g., Linux) and other Internet Access Providers (LAP) offerings (e.g., alternative Internet connections such as AOL) launch at boot-up.[9]

2. Increased flexibility for third party IT companies

Like OEMs, ISVs and Independent Hardware Vendors (IHVs) gain the flexibility to develop, distribute, use, sell, or license any software that competes with Windows or Microsoft middleware without restrictions or any kind of retaliation from Microsoft.[10] The importance of this fact cannot be overstated. ISVs and IHVs, especially the thousands of small and mid-size companies in these categories, make up a bulk of the IT industry and will be able to utilize this flexi-

---

[3] *United States v. Microsoft*, 253 F.3d 34 (D.C. Cir. 2001) at 102.

[4] The Court of Appeals noted "Because plaintiffs have not carried their burden on either prong, [of an attempted monopolization analysis] we reverse without remand." *Id.*, at 63.

[5] "Microsoft Middleware Product" is a defined term, while inconsistent with common industry usage, has the meaning of "the functionality provided by Internet Explorer, Microsoft's Java Virtual Machine, Windows Media Player, Windows Messenger, Outlook Express and their successors in a Windows Operating System Product." Revised Proposed Final Judgment, Section VI.K.

[6] Id., Section III.A.

[7] Id., Section III.G.

[8] Id., Section III.C.

[9] Id., Section III.C.

[10] Id., Section III.F.

bility to innovate and deliver "consumer critical" products such as instant messaging and digital media to consumers.

The ISVs and IHVs will obtain advance disclosure of Windows APIs, communications protocols, which will increase the quantity and quality of competitive product offerings.[11] As with OEMs, Microsoft will be barred from thwarting competition by entering into agreements that obligate ISVs, IHVs, IAPs, or ICPs to any exclusive or fixed-percentage arrangements.[12] It should be noted that the settlement restricts some freedoms in crafting contracts with Microsoft, and thus may discourage some companies that might otherwise like to sign on to "dance" with Microsoft. However, it also protects other companies from any efforts by Microsoft to prevent them from teaming up with Microsoft's competitors like Sun Microsystems or AOL.

3. Greater consumer choice

Nothing is as important to our industry as giving consumers, or end users, the freedom to choose what products and services they want or need. To this end, the settlement ensures that consumers will have the ability to enable or remove access to Microsoft or non-Microsoft middleware, or substitute a non-Microsoft middleware product for a Microsoft middleware product for a Microsoft middleware product.[13] Microsoft's detractors have generated much commotion with the notion that removal of icons or "automatic invocations" is not enough, and that to give consumers "real" choice, underlying code would have to be removed. This is nonsensical for two reasons. First, it is a known fact that removal of visible access (e.g., an icon) to middleware or an application is a very effective means of getting the end user to forget about it. Think about how many icons reside on the average user's desktop that serve to "remind" him of what product to use for a certain task. It is a simple case of "out of sight, out of mind." Second, it is also a known fact that removal of the underlying does nothing to enhance consumer choice, and actually could destabilize the platform, increasing costs to consumer software developers who could no longer count on programming interfaces within the Windows operating system. The net result of these provisions is that consumers will be in the position to pick the products *they* consider to best meet their needs—whether it be downloading music, sharing pictures over the Web, or chatting with friends via instant messaging applications.

Another myth propagated by Microsoft's competitors is that Microsoft gets to reset the desktop to its preferred configuration 14 days after the consumer buys it no matter what steps the OEM or the consumer have actually taken to try to exercise the choice to use a non-Microsoft product. This is absolutely false. The desktop would not be reset and consumers will always retain choice. For example, consumers can choose among the OEM's configuration, their own configuration and Microsoft's configuration.

4. Effective Enforcement

The final element of the settlement that will ensure competition is the enforcement provisions. Microsoft must license its intellectual property to the extent necessary for OEMs and other IT companies to exercise any of the flexibility provided in the agreement.[14] In an unprecedented move, the decree creates a jointly appointed Technical Committee (TC) to monitor compliance.[15] The TC will have three members and unspecified staff, and be granted unfettered access to Microsoft staff and documents. While the TC is a better enforcement mechanism than having to apply to a court for each software design element, it is not without some flaws. For example, there are no restrictions on how the TC can be utilized as a tool by Microsoft's competitors to delay shipment of an operating system or middleware product. While this may cause Microsoft some heartburn if it is used for such delay, it will be a fatal malady to the thousands of small and mid-size ISVs, IHVs, training firms and consultants that depend on a timely product launch. I am not a lawyer, so I can only propose a practical solution to this problem. Perhaps the competitors (or anyone else with the view that Microsoft is not complying with the consent decree) should be required to bring their problems to the TC at specified times during the development life cycle. This would prevent "last minute" delays.

[11] Id., Sections III.D., III.E.
[12] Id., Sections III.G., III.F.
[13] Id. III.H.
[14] Id., Section III.I.
[15] Id., Section IV.B.

Finally, Microsoft is required to implement an internal Compliance Officer to be responsible for handling complaints and compliance issues.[16] This is yet another safeguard that aggrieved parties can use to ensure Microsoft's compliance with the consent decree.

Unfortunately these provisions are not enough to satiate some bent on seeing that this settlement never gets approved. For example, they question why the settlement lasts for only 5 years rather than the customary 10. This inquiry fails to acknowledge the realities of the IT industry and the speed at which we innovate. One need only think about the number and types of products that have emerged since 1998 to see why applying static conduct restrictions are out of step with our industry and provide no added value. Further, I believe seeking extended application of the settlement only exposes a bias against Microsoft

Because of the significant impact on our industry, I must also address the additional remedies proposed by the nine state attorneys general who did not sign the consent decree. While their aim to "restore competition" is a valid and important antitrust principle—as long as it is limited to the elimination of competitive barriers—their proposal ignores the Court of Appeals ruling and runs counter to established antitrust jurisprudence. The DOJ settlement agreement was wise to avoid the dangerous temptation to redesign and regulate market outcomes. I'll point out two defects of the state's proposal. First, requiring that Windows "must carry" Java does *nothing* for consumers who can download it with one click and only serves to thwart competition by giving Sun Microsystems a special government-mandated monopoly with which other middleware companies will have to compete. While I believe "must-carry" provisions are inherently anticompetitive, if the attorneys general were really trying to stand on principle they would have to ask for the same provisions for other middleware providers as well. Second, requiring Microsoft to port its Office product to Linux is tantamount to making it a "ward of the state." There are already several office productivity suites available to users of Linux and some are even free. It would stand to reason that if attorneys general are actually interested in removing any "applications barrier to entry" that may exist, they should force the developers of ALL popular software products to port them to Linux. It is clear that from the extreme nature of these proposals that the settlement must encompass all reasonable mechanisms to restore competition. The respondents to the Voter Consumer Research polls mentioned above also question the need for the far-reaching remedies that would hamper Microsoft's ability to innovate. In Utah for example, nearly 70% of voters believe that Microsoft's products have helped consumers and over 80% of these voters feel that that Microsoft has benefited the computer industry. These numbers beg the question: Where's the harm that would justify the nine state's harsh remedies.

Conclusion

For ACT member companies, the IT industry and for me, it has been a very long three and a half years. This settlement reflects a balanced resolution to this litigation and a welcome end to the uncertainty that has hung over our industry at a time when certainty is what we need most. It addresses the anticompetitive actions articulated by a unanimous Court of Appeals. I believe Assistant Attorney Charles James when he said "This settlement . . . has the advantages of immediacy and certainty."[17] It my sincere hope that the District Court will approve the settlement at the conclusion of the public comment period. There is no doubt in my mind that it is in the public interest to do so.

Again, I thank the Committee for the opportunity to include the views of ACT's member companies at this important hearing.

[16] Id., Section IV.C.

[17] Remarks of Assistant Attorney Charles James, Department of Justice press conference, November 2, 2001.

THE BARKSDALE GROUP

James L. Barksdale
jimb@barksdalegroup.com
(650) 234 5252

December 11, 2001

The Honorable Patrick J. Leahy
Chairman
Committee on the Judiciary
United States Senate
SD-224
Washington, D.C. 20510

The Honorable Orrin G. Hatch
Ranking Minority Member
Committee on the Judiciary
United States Senate
SD-224
Washington, D.C. 20510

Dear Chairman Leahy and Senator Hatch,

I was privileged to have received the invitation to testify at your hearing on Wednesday, December 12, and had looked forward to offering my views about the likely effect of the proposed Microsoft settlement, particularly on the state of innovation in the high-technology industries.

At the time I was asked to testify, it was suggested my testimony might be useful to the committee because of my experience as the CEO of Netscape, and especially because Netscape was founded at a time when Microsoft was first charged with Sherman Act violations. Those of us at Netscape competed with Microsoft at a time when Microsoft was theoretically constrained by a 1995 Consent Decree, and thus I would be in a position to attest to Microsoft's business conduct during a period in which anticompetitive actions would theoretically be restrained.

Moreover, my testimony would have been free of any fear of Microsoft. I am no longer in a business that competes with them. I can afford to tell the truth, and the truth needs to be told.

It is an established legal fact that Microsoft has retaliated against firms like Netscape, Intel, Apple, Real Networks, IBM, Compaq and a host of others which have

2730 Sand Hill Road Suite 100, Menlo Park, CA 94025
(650) 234 5200 main (650) 234 5201 fax
www.barksdalegroup.com ideas@barksdalegroup.com

The Honorable Patrick J. Leahy
The Honorable Orrin G. Hatch
December 11, 2001
Page 2

deigned to compete with parts of Microsoft's business. The courts have repeatedly and unanimously found that this atmosphere has led to the stifling of innovation throughout the high-technology sector, harming consumers and the economy. Perhaps worse, Microsoft has created an atmosphere where those who witness violations of the law are afraid to share what they know with law enforcement officials. The certainty of retaliation against these potential witnesses has had, to varying degrees, the effect of obstructing justice. One of the points I would have made had I been able to testify is that the settlement between Microsoft and the Department of Justice would do virtually nothing to protect computer manufacturers and others from Microsoft's retaliation. Which means that, fundamentally, Microsoft's behavior will not be changed by it. The settlement is simply that – a memorial to the end, not a remedy for the past or for the future.

Over the last five years, the Committee has pushed software companies to step forward and make public their concerns about Microsoft's illegal conduct, to identify how the company's anticompetitive behavior was eliminating competition, discouraging investment and stifling innovation. Witnesses were told – and I was one of them – that policymakers understood that antitrust law enforcement was critical to insuring competition in the software industry. Witnesses were told that cooperation with the government not only made good business sense; it was their public duty, and necessary to insure the illegal conduct was appropriately remedied.

Not surprisingly, many were reluctant, fearful of what would happen to their businesses and their employees. Many that came forward paid a heavy price. Retaliation was meted out in a variety of ways. Meanwhile, the company that broke the law has only grown stronger. The Committee may wish to consider how this result might impact the administration of justice, as well as any potential future testimony in both the legislative and judicial branches of government.

During the Cold War, we used to refer to a concept known as Finlandization. What this referred to was that Finland was nominally free of the Soviet Union, but was so threatened by it, it could not act unilaterally without tempering its actions so as not to offend its giant neighbor which could crush it at will. The technology industry now, and after the settlement with DOJ, is still effectively, Finlandized by Microsoft. It is still dominated, and will still cower in fear of the monopolist unbound. The resolution of the antitrust litigation will to a large degree determine whether or when that atmosphere changes. That may well be a larger issue than the specifics of any proposed settlement. I note with some real satisfaction that the remedy outlined last Friday by the nine state Attorneys General who remain as plaintiffs would have the effect of genuinely constraining Microsoft, and thus liberating the technology industry from the shadow cast by Microsoft.

The Honorable Patrick J. Leahy
The Honorable Orrin G. Hatch
December 11, 2001
Page 3

These developments have stiffened my resolve to do all that I can to insure that competition and consumer choice are reintroduced to the industry. It is vitally important that no company can do to a future Netscape what Microsoft did to Netscape from 1995 to 1999. It is universally recognized that that the 1995 Consent Decree was ineffective. I respectfully submit that the Proposed Final Judgment ("PFJ"), which is the subject of the hearing, will be even less effective, if possible, than the 1995 Decree in restoring competition and stopping anticompetitive behavior.

Accordingly, Senator Leahy, I am going to follow your suggestion that I help the committee answer one of the central questions:

If the PFJ had been in effect all along, how would it have affected Netscape? More important, how will it affect future Netscapes?

Impact on future Netscapes.

As discussed in the attached document, the unambiguous conclusion is that if the PFJ agreed upon last month by Microsoft and the Department of Justice had been in existence in 1994, Netscape would have never been able to obtain the necessary venture capital financing. In fact, the company would not have come into being in the first place. The work of Marc Andreesen's team at the University of Illinois in developing the Mosaic browser would likely have remained an academic exercise.

An innovative, independent browser company simply could not survive under the PFJ. And such would be the effect on any company developing in the future technologies as innovative as the browser was in the mid 1990s.

That leaves the question of whether Microsoft itself would have developed browser technology necessary for Internet navigation. My belief is that Microsoft would not have developed that technology. It is abundantly clear that Microsoft viewed the browser and the Internet itself as the principal threat to their core business of selling operating systems and applications for desktop computers.

This PFJ allows Microsoft to employ the full fury of its multiple monopolies against anyone who would develop a browser or any other technology that might have the potential to challenge any aspects of Microsoft's business. I have reviewed the PFJ, and my impression continues to be that it is a document whose principal purpose is to protect Microsoft from competition, and not to open up the market to competition with Microsoft. I note, again with pleasure, that the remedy proposal by the state Attorneys General who remain as plaintiffs would significantly open the market up to competition.

The Honorable Patrick J. Leahy
The Honorable Orrin G. Hatch
December 11, 2001
Page 4

If the PFJ provisions are allowed to go into effect, it is unrealistic to think that anybody would ever secure venture capital financing to compete against Microsoft. This would be a tragedy for our nation. It makes a mockery of the notion that the PFJ is "good for the economy."

If the PFJ goes into effect, it will subject an entire industry to dominance by an unconstrained monopolist, thus snuffing out competition, consumer choice and innovation in perhaps our nation's most important industry. And worse, it will allow them to extend their dominance to more traditional businesses such as financial services, entertainment, telecommunications, and perhaps many others.

Four years ago I appeared before the committee and was able to demonstrate, with the help of the audience, that Microsoft undoubtedly had a monopoly. Now it has been proven in the courts that Microsoft not only has a monopoly, but they have illegally maintained that monopoly through a series of abusive and predatory actions. I submit to the committee that Microsoft is infinitely stronger in each of their core businesses than they were four years ago, despite the fact that their principal arguments have been repudiated 8-0 by the federal courts.

I hope you will keep these thoughts in mind during your hearings.

A more detailed analysis of my views follows.

Sincerely yours,

James L. Barksdale

JLB/s
Attachment

Background on Netscape and the Internet browser.

Many of you know that Netscape was founded by Dr. Jim Clark and Marc Andreesen. Marc had been a participant in National Science Foundation programs in the early 90s at the University of Illinois, where he and his team in 1993 wrote the code that became the first easy to use browser. Even though the Internet and its ancestors had been around since the 1960's, the graphical browser – which allowed non-computer scientists to navigate the Internet - was the technological innovation we had been waiting for. This led to the creation of Netscape in 1994. This triggered an explosion of innovation, and changed all of our lives. I am proud to have served as Netscape's CEO from 1995-1999, when it was acquired by AOL, and very proud of the role Netscape had in changing the world for the better.

A. API Disclosure. The browser was and is a third party application. But it was also a potential platform which exposed Application Programming Interfaces ("APIs") and supported other third party applications. Third party applications writers desired to write applications to the browser platform, because once these applications worked with the browser, they would automatically run on any operating system on which the browser was present. It is well documented that Microsoft was concerned this phenomenon would commoditize Windows – meaning that this would bring about real competition in the operating system market. Introducing competition to a monopolized market would have been exactly the kind of positive development our competition policies welcome.

Of course, the browser could not work without an operating system. We needed Microsoft's cooperation and we needed the Windows APIs necessary to insure Netscape's browser interoperated with Windows.

It was well known that Windows '95 would be a major product release for Microsoft. We contacted Microsoft in the spring of 1995 about obtaining the necessary APIs, the same APIs they were distributing to other 3rd party applications writers. Because Microsoft viewed Netscape as a potential competitor, they withheld the necessary APIs from Netscape for an extended period of time – almost a year.

Question 1. Would the PFJ have compelled the disclosure of the APIs necessary for Netscape's browser to interoperate with Windows?

Answer: A resounding no. The PFJ would not have compelled meaningful disclosure in a timely way.

It is advertised that the PFJ "requires" Microsoft to disclose to third party software developers the APIs for Windows. A review of the definitions reveals that the provision is essentially meaningless. APIs for new versions of the Windows operating systems must be disclosed in a "timely manner." "Timely manner" is triggered when Microsoft distributes beta copies of its software to 150,000 "beta testers." It is highly doubtful Microsoft ever distributed beta copies of its software to 150,000 "beta testers". More important, this provision allows Microsoft to unilaterally decide not to reach the timely manner definition in the first place, which insures they can avoid disclosure by simply keeping the number of beta testers remains below 150,000.

The other disclosure requirements in the PFJ seem to call for the kind of disclosure made to members of the Microsoft Developers Network. The problem of withholding necessary APIs only presents itself when the entity requesting the APIs is a partial competitor to Microsoft. Under the PFJ, Microsoft's ability to arbitrarily withhold APIs from those that would deign to enter into competition with Microsoft is left intact.

Moreover, provision J of the Proposed Final Judgment allows Microsoft to withhold technical information if it might "compromise the security" of authentication or encryption systems. This provision would clearly implicate information disclosed relevant to browser technology, since a browser, by definition, encapsulates encryption software. The Committee needs to understand that products either interoperate or they don't. In order to interoperate effectively, third parties must have all of the information, not some subset defined by Microsoft.

For example, in 1995, there was a debate between Microsoft and Netscape about whose authentication and encryption software was better. Netscape had developed and implemented SSL, and Microsoft had implemented SMTP. Microsoft would have never distributed APIs at a critical time in Netscape's development because they could have claimed, if the PFJ had been in effect, those APIs would undermine SMTP.

Lastly, the PFJ fails to define the critical term "interoperability." The PFJ leaves the term to be defined by Microsoft.

The sum of the API provision will ensure that Microsoft will continue to determine the flow of information to third party developers. And any dispute – which may be favorably resolved by the so-called "Technical Committee," will never be conducted in a timely manner.

B. <u>Killing browser competition by commingling browser code with Windows and calling it all "Windows".</u>

Netscape distributed the first commercially successful browser. Microsoft decided to distribute their browsers without charge. As the litigation demonstrated, Microsoft decided by 1997 to bolt the browser together with Windows because, as their testimony indicated, they were losing the battle.

Litigation ensued. Microsoft denied that it had violated the law in so doing, citing the language of the 1995 Consent Decree. Ultimately, the Court of Appeals held in June, 1998, that under the terms of the 1995 Consent Decree, Microsoft was entitled to bind products together as long as there was a "facially plausible" explanation for having done so. The Court pointedly said at the time that this issue might have been decided differently if it were a Sherman Act case rather than a Consent Decree case. Nevertheless, Microsoft seized upon this Consent Decree opinion and claimed that it could now bundle a ham sandwich as part of Windows if they wanted.

Let me make one point clear: while I believe this was the wrong result, I do not blame Microsoft for attempting to prevail on this point. The fault lies with the Department of Justice for having written a poor agreement with Microsoft in the first place. The agreement was flawed in that it contained language which was at best ambiguous and, at worst, an avenue for Microsoft to flaunt the decree.

The Sherman Act antitrust case against Microsoft was filed in May, 1998. The government alleged that Microsoft's practice of tying the browser and operating system together was illegal. In June, 2001, the Court of Appeals this time said that Microsoft's practice of "commingling" the browser and operating system code together was illegal.

Question 2. How does the PFJ deal with the issue of binding other software to Windows?

Answer. Remarkably, the PFJ adopts Microsoft's ham sandwich argument. It contains a definition which says that Windows is whatever Microsoft says it is. The net effect of this is whenever any software is developed which could threaten Microsoft, Microsoft can simply bolt a similar product into Windows and call it all one product. Since this language is more favorable to Microsoft than current law, it is an example of how Microsoft, the defendant in the lawsuit, actually gained affirmative exceptions from current law through negotiations with the Department of Justice.

Once again, I don't blame Microsoft for trying. They're supposed to negotiate the best deal possible. It is the fault of the Justice Department and the various states who agreed to this.

The PFJ not only would not have protected Netscape from Microsoft's predatory conduct. It actually would have provided less protection than any of the legal standards that have existed the past ten years.

C. Distribution and Retaliation. The most important distribution channel in the software business is the OEM channel. Microsoft controls that channel by virtue of having the Windows monopoly. If Microsoft chooses not to distribute Windows to a particular OEM in a timely manner, the OEM simply cannot sell computers.

The OEM channel became the most important distribution channel for Netscape as well. Microsoft used its market power to impede Netscape's ability to distribute browsers. They said they were going to "choke off (our) air supply" and they began to execute on that strategy. OEMs who wanted to feature Netscape's browser were punished by Microsoft. The price of Windows was increased, or the threat of cancelling the Windows license was made.

Question 3. How does the PFJ protect against retaliation by Microsoft against an OEM or anybody else who would prefer to feature or sell non-Microsoft software?

Answer: The first thing that must be taken into account is that there is nothing in this remedy which will lead to more competition in the operating system market, so OEMs know that Microsoft's position is more secure as a monopolist than ever before. That fact, juxtaposed with the permanent cancellation threat Microsoft gained by this settlement, is intended to and will freeze any OEM wishing to promote non-Microsoft alternatives. Under this agreement, Microsoft can terminate, without notice, a PC companies Windows license, after sending the PC company two notices that it believes it is violating its license. There need not be any adjudication or determination by any independent tribunal that Microsoft's claims are correct; only two notices to any PC company of a putative violation, and thereafter, Microsoft may terminate *without even giving notice*. This provision means that the PC companies are, at any time, just two registered letters away from an unannounced economic calamity. It will render the PC companies severely limited in their willingness to promote products that compete with Microsoft.

Even though Microsoft is an adjudged monopolist, it is constrained only from certain specified forms of retaliation, presumably empowering it to engage in other forms of retaliation. This formulation is particularly problematic because the protected PC company activities are narrowly and specifically defined. Retaliation against a PC company for installing a non-Microsoft application that does not meet the middleware definition is NOT prohibited; nor is retaliation against a PC company for removing a MSFT application that does not meet the middleware definition.

Microsoft can price Windows at a high price, and then put economic pressure on the PC company to use only Microsoft applications through the provision that Microsoft can provide unlimited consideration to PC companies for distributing or promoting Microsoft's services or products. The limitation that these payments must be "commensurate with the absolute level or amount of" PC company expenditures is hollow, since there is no cost methodology proposed, and no mechanism to account for costs in any event.

Under the settlement, Microsoft can provide unlimited "market development allowances, programs, or other discounts in connection with Windows Operating System Products." This provision essentially eviscerates the entire scheme of PC company choice, functioning the same way as the rebate provision discussed above, but without any tether or limiting principle whatsoever. Simply put, MSFT can charge $150 per copy of Windows, but then provide a $99 "market development allowance" for PC companies that install Windows Media Player as opposed to Real Networks media player.

Presumably, this is intend to be prescribed by a provision which says that "discounts or their award" shall not be "based on or impose any criterion or requirement that is otherwise inconsistent with ... this Final Judgment," but this circular and self-referential provision does not ensure that the practice identified above is prohibited

And Microsoft is free to retaliate against PC companies that promote competition by withholding any existing form of "non-monetary Compensation" – only "newly introduced forms of non-monetary Consideration" may not be withheld.

Note that the Wall Street article of December 10 by John Wilke, which discussed why computer makers would not testify before the Senate Judiciary Committee: "None of the computer makers that are supposed to be the chief beneficiaries of the Justice Department settlement agreed to testify. Two major computer makers said in interviews that the proposed settlement's antiretaliation provisions are so weak that they were unlikely to take advantage of its other provisions allowing PC makers to use rival technologies. The government settlement 'leaves Microsoft as the gatekeeper of innovation in the industry,' an executive of one PC maker said last week.

Remember that we are talking about the remedy in antitrust case where the monopolist has been found to have violated the law in spades. Ask yourselves how it is possible that in this remedy Microsoft secured for itself the right to retaliate against anybody.

D. Allowing consumers to exercise real software choice. We believed at Netscape that as long as consumers could exercise real browser choice, Netscape could compete with Microsoft. We even said we could "compete with free". That is, a scenario where our customers paid for browsers and Microsoft gave its browser away for free. We ultimately were unable to compete with a free product that was bolted to the operating system for anticompetitive reasons.

Question 4. Does the PFJ empower the consumer to make choices about what software to use, and if so, does it require Microsoft to respect those choices in the future?

Two of the key provisions of the PFJ cited by DOJ as instrumental in restoring competition merely require Microsoft continue to engage in business as usual. First, DOJ points to the provision that allows PC companies and end users to remove "end user access" to Microsoft middleware (i.e. Internet Explorer, Windows Media Player, Windows Messenger, etc). It is important to understand that all "end user access" really means is the ability to remove the "icon" for the middleware application, not the middleware itself. Second, DOJ "grants" the PC companies "flexibility" to add or remove icons on the Windows desktop.

We have been down this road before. OEMs will not exercise choice to merely remove or add icons because that is not a meaningful choice. PC companies have always enjoyed the flexibility to add icons to the Windows desktop. Microsoft specifically announced in July that OEMs could remove Internet Explorer icons from the desktop. And Microsoft had previously been ordered by the Court to display such flexibility in 1998. Until the fundamental relationship between Microsoft and the OEMs changes, no OEM will avail themselves of this cosmetic flexibility.

Astonishingly, Microsoft actually secured for itself in the PFJ a provision that allows Microsoft to exploit its "desktop sweeper" to eliminate PC company installed icons by asking an end user if he/she wants the PC company-installed configuration wiped out after 14 days. Thus, the PC company flexibility provisions will only last on the desktop with certainty for 14 days, and after that period, persistent automated queries from Microsoft can reverse the effect of the PC company's installations. The effect of this provision is to severely devalue the ability of PC companies to offer premier desktop space to ISVs – and to undermine the ability of PC companies to differentiate their products and provide consumers with real choices.

So, under this remedy, Microsoft gets to undermine the choices made by PC companies and grants Microsoft a second, third, and truly, infinite bites at the apple, to badger consumers into -- unknowingly or unwittingly – switching back to Microsoft's software.

The add/remove provisions in the agreement only allow for removal of end user access to Microsoft middleware, not the middleware itself. For example, a PC company or a consumer might choose to eliminate Microsoft's Internet Explorer and replace it with Netscape's Navigator as the default. Under this provision, Microsoft's Internet Explorer – not Netscape's Navigator – is still used in the MyDocuments, MyMusic, MyPictures and Windows Explorer folders. So Microsoft has secured an agreement that insures that Internet Explorer is used even when a consumer has chosen otherwise. And as stated above, Microsoft has secured in this agreement insurance that its browser and other middleware remains on PCs, even if the icon is removed. That will have the effect of guaranteeing that applications writers would not write to Netscape's browser.

As we have seen with the implementation of this approach (i.e., icon removal only) with regard to Internet Explorer in Windows XP, MSFT can use the presentation of this option in the utility to make it less desirable to end users.

And remarkable, the agreement gives Microsoft a new weapon to use in its war to preserve the desktop as its own: it can demand that PC companies include icons for non-MSFT middleware in the add/remove utility.

Ask yourself this: we are talking about a remedy that flows from a case where Microsoft has brazenly violated antitrust laws. Why in the world should Microsoft be able to secure for itself in this remedy a provision that allows consumers to remove non-Microsoft software? This treats the other companies as if they broke the law, not Microsoft.

CONCLUSION: These are just a few of the provisions that would have affected Netscape or a similar company attempting to have a successful browser business. As stated above, it is my belief that if these provisions had been in effect, it is highly unlikely Netscape would have ever been founded.

If these provisions are allowed to go into effect, no entity will be able to secure venture capital financing to compete against Microsoft in any aspect of its business.

Policymakers must understand the consequences of this proposed action. I regret not being able to share my views directly with the Senate Judiciary Committee, but trust that you will do the necessary due diligence before this badly flawed agreement goes forward in the courts. The policy signal that will be sent if this agreement is finalized is that particularly determined monopolists will be rewarded for their intransigence. Is that really the competition policy of this country?

Statement of Robert H. Bork, Washington, D.C.

Dear Chairman Leahy and Senator Hatch:

The Proposed Final Judgment (PFJ) in *U.S. v. Microsoft* is a woefully inadequate end to more than 11 years of investigation and litigation against Microsoft Corporation. There is no longer a debate over Microsoft's liability under the antitrust laws. Microsoft has been found liable before the District Court. Microsoft lost its appeal to the United States Court of Appeals for the District of Columbia Circuit sitting *en banc* in a 7–0 decision. Microsoft's petition for a rehearing before the Court of Appeals was refused. Microsoft's petition for *certiorari* before the Supreme Court was also denied. The courts have decided that Microsoft possesses monopoly power and has used that power unlawfully to protect its monopoly.

The case now turns back to the District Court for review under the Antitrust Procedures and Penalties Act—the so-called Tunney Act. Under the Tunney Act the Court must reach an independent judgment on whether or not the settlement is in the "public interest." The District Court finds itself in an interesting posture in that in the 30 years since the Tunney Act was enacted, it has never been applied in a case which has been litigated and affirmed. What is unique about the application of the Tunney Act in *U.S. v. Microsoft* is that rather than some ambiguous "public interest" standard, the District Court will now be obligated to reach a decision on whether or not the settlement corresponds to the clear guidance of the Court of Appeals.

The court of appeals set out a simple standard for measuring the legal sufficiency of any remedy selected in the *Microsoft* litigation: the remedy must "seek to 'unfetter [the] market from anticompetitive conduct,' * * * to 'terminate the illegal monopoly, deny to the defendant the fruits of its statutory violation, and ensure that there remain no practices likely to result in monopolization in the future.'" *United States v. Microsoft Corp.*, 253 F.3d 34, 103 (D.C. Cir. 2001) (*"Microsoft III"*) (*quoting Ford Motor Co. v. United States*, 405 U.S. 562, 577 (1972), and *United States v. United Shoe Machinery Corp.*, 391 U.S. 244, 250 (1968)). The Court of Appeals was very deliberate in its handling of this case, and its finely crafted opinion manifestly chose its words and precedents with care. In citing the *Ford Autolite* and *United Shoe* cases, the D.C. Circuit underscored the clear guidance of the Supreme Court in monopolization cases.

The D.C. Circuit provided equally straightforward guidance in explaining Microsoft's liability for illegal monopolization. At the core of the case was Microsoft's successful campaign to eliminate the dual threats of Netscape's Navigator web browser and the Java programming language. Both Navigator and Java were "platform threats" to Microsoft's underlying operating system. Both Navigator and Nava served as "middleware." "Middleware" means that these programs exposed applications programming interfaces (APIs) so that third party applications developers could write applications to Navigator and Java in lieu of the underlying Windows operating system. And because both Navigator and Java ran on operating systems other than Windows they fundamentally threatened the Windows operating system, Microsoft's core source of monopoly power. The D.C. Circuit could not have been clearer on these points. See *Microsoft III*, 253 F.3d at 53–56. 60. At a minimum any proposed settlement must effectively remedy this problem.

Unfortunately, the remedy accepted by the Antitrust Division of the Justice Department ignores most of the key findings by both the Court of Appeals and the District Court. The PFJ falls far short of the standards for relief clearly articulated by the Court of Appeals and the United States Supreme Court. The PFJ includes provisions that potentially make the competitive landscape of the software industry worse. And, the PFJ contains so many ambiguities and loopholes as to make it unenforceable, and likely to guarantee years of additional litigation.

That the PFJ will hamper Microsoft's illegal behavior not at all is shown by the reactions of the investment community:

"We have review the Settlement Agreement between MSFT and the DOJ . . . the states (and to a lesser degree the DoJ) had talked tough and set expectations for a knock-out victory, and now must accept criticism that they walked away with too little concessions from Microsoft." Goldman Sachs, 11/2/01

"As we have stated before, we believe a settlement is a best case scenario for Microsoft. And, this settlement in particular seems like a win for Microsoft being that it would preserve Microsoft's ability to bundle its Internet assets with Windows XP and future operating systems—a plus for the company. In fact, it appears that Internet assets such as Passport are untouched. Also, as is typical with legal judgments, this settlement is backward looking, not forward looking. In other words, it looks at processes in the past, but not potential development of the future." Morgan Stanley, 11/02/01

"The deal . . . appears to be 'more, better, and faster' than we expected in a settlement deal between Microsoft and DoJ. The deal will apparently require few if any changes in Windows XP and leave important aspects of Microsoft's market power intact." Prudential Financial, 11/01/01

"With a dramatic win last week, Microsoft appears to be on its way to putting the U.S. antitrust case behind it. The PFJ between the Department of Justice and Microsoft gives little for Microsoft's competitors to cheer about. . . . There is very little chance that competitors could prove or win effective relief from violation of this agreement, in our view." Schwab Capital Markets, 11/6/01

This takes on particular importance given the state of the software market. Since the end of the trial before the District Court the market has changed substantially:

- Microsoft's monopolies *are stronger* in each of its core markets with both the Windows operating system and the Office suite now higher than 92 percent and 95 percent, respectively;
- Microsoft has achieved a *new monopoly* in web browsers;
- Competitive forces that may have existed in the past—most notably the Linux operating system—now clearly pose no threat to Microsoft's monopoly; and
- Microsoft has made clear it intends to further protect and extend its monopoly through a series of initiatives including, Hailstorm (web-services); Windows XP, and .NET.

Some policy makers have adopted the view that settling this case could somehow revive the slowing U.S. economy. This is an absurd proposition. The problem with the PC sector today is that demand has slowed and prices for PC hardware have plummeted (as opposed to Microsoft's software which has effectively increased in price). It is simply incorrect to equate slowing PC demand with Microsoft's legal problems. Also, we are unaware of any economic theory that suggests that monopolies maintained by predatory conduct—as opposed to competition and innovation—can spur economic growth. As the Precursor Group recently pointed out: "investor lament about the lack of broadband and the absence of killer applications is the 'other side of the coin' to investor glee with the market power and profits of incumbent Bell, Cable, and Microsoft monopolies . . . having legal monopolies on the major access points to the Internet is unlikely to maximize innovation and growth that investors are counting on."

The briefing memorandum offered in support of these views documents general problems with the PFJ and specific section-by-section analysis of the PFJ's provisions. However, this memorandum is meant to be illustrative—not comprehensive—to give policy makers a preview of the issues to be examined under the Tunney Act. The Antitrust Division and Microsoft will continue to insist that the PFJ sufficiently remedies the issues in the case.

Yet these arguments simply cannot be squared with the fact that every independent investment analyst and industry analyst has concluded that this remedy will have *no* material impact on Microsoft's business.

Policy makers also need to pay attention to the precedent this case establishes. In settling the most important antitrust case in decades through a remedy that will have not impact on the current or future competitive landscape, and absolutely no deterrent effect on the defendant, the Department of Justice has effectively repealed a major segment of the nation's antitrust laws. Moreover, any potential witness with knowledge of anticompetitive conduct in a monopolized market has to weigh the potential benefit of his or her testimony against the likely response of the defendant monopolist. The DOJ's proposed meaningless remedy would insure that no witness would ever testify against Microsoft in any future enforcement action.

The PFJ, in short, places this defendant in a position of effectively being above the antitrust laws, and does so by surrendering the government's victory in the District Court and the unanimous seven-member Court of Appeals. That is a result that should not be countenanced.

Statement of Jerry Hilburn, President and Founder, Catfish Software, Inc., San Diego, California

I am very pleased to provide a written statement for your hearing on "The Microsoft Settlement: A Look to the Future." Thank you, Chairman Leahy and Members of the Committee, for the opportunity to deliver a small businessperson's perspective on the case before this distinguished group.

I would like to tell you my point of view on the Microsoft case. I am a small businessman in San Diego, California. Catfish Software, Inc. started operations in 1994 providing network services and custom database applications for small business. In 1998, Catfish Software launched an E-mail Application Services branch providing double opt-in mail list service and web-based customer support applications and today, Catfish Software provides support to 300+ companies reaching 2,000,000+ subscribers of its software services.

One of my firm's top competitors is Microsoft's bCentral. So you may ask why I speak in favor of the Microsoft settlement.

Businesses large and small have mortgaged their futures against the impact of the terrorist war. Some smaller businesses—technology and otherwise—have already found themselves strangled by a lack of consumer demand and by slowdowns in corporate and consumer spending. Most of us are finding it is time to shore up resources and protect our assets from the impact of the war.

In this time of so much uncertainty, we need the promise of a brighter day and the knowledge that the government—from the federal level on down—is doing everything possible to invigorate our flagging economy.

Competition and consumer preference should decide the direction of the marketplace and meanwhile, the government should not rush to intervene in the New Economy. The last thing our economy needs at this time is the burden of remedies which do nothing but slow the pace of development and limit the choices of consumers.

The Justice Department handled this case admirably, and the settlement they agreed upon is sound. The settlement outlines how Microsoft can operate, but more importantly it provides some assurances to an industry that has been on unstable ground lately.

Microsoft's ability to design and produce new software in turn creates opportunities for small and medium-sized developers to write applications which operate on a Windows-based platform.

As the old saying goes, a high tide floats all ships. Calls for break-up of the company did not help the already tenuous situation. And when Microsoft looked like it might be pulled under, the Nasdaq was hit as well as the stocks of many high-tech companies.

But when announcements of the settlement were made public around the beginning of November 2001, everyone got a nice little bump. Consumers and other technology entrepreneurs were hopeful that this case could be put to bed and that the tech sector could get back to business.

This litigation that has been an albatross around all our necks for so long—and ending the string of lawsuits associated with it—will have a positive effect on the tech economy. With a little luck, that will ripple out to America's economy as a whole.

With so many technologies poised to enter the marketplace, Microsoft and many others, including Catfish Software are looking for ways to enhance the computing experience. The Internet has become a center of most everyone's daily lives—from toddlers typing their first strokes with learning games to seniors learning how to send and receive e-mail. Untapped markets and unimagined ideas abound, but we must not harness the creativity or the ability of software firms to bring those products to bear in the marketplace.

The olive branch of settlement was extended, and it is a solution that is good for the economy and good for the tech industry. Allow us the opportunity to get back to work and earn money with our products and ideas once again.

This concludes my testimony. Once again, I thank the Committee and its distinguished Members for the opportunity to provide written testimony on this important issue.

Statement of the Computing Technology Industry Association, Washington, D.C.

STATEMENT OF INTEREST

The Computing Technology Industry Association (CompTIA) is the world's largest trade association in the information technology and communications sector. CompTIA represents over 8,000 hardware and software manufacturers, distributors, retailers, Internet, telecommunications, IT training and other service companies in over 50 countries. The overwhelming majority of CompTIA members are resellers—companies that resell software and hardware to consumers, businesses, or other resellers. These resellers are vendor-neutral and their objective is to be able to sell whatever products their customers wish to buy. In that sense they believe that antitrust laws should focus primarily on consumer impact rather than competitor impact. Microsoft is a member of CompTIA as are many of Microsoft's competitors.

In 1998, CompTIA's Board of Directors adopted a formal policy statement on antitrust. That statement supports sensible antitrust enforcement that is based on demonstrable economic effects in the marketplace. CompTIA believes that market forces typically correct any temporary market imperfections and that government regulators should only intervene in the technology marketplace when there is overwhelming evidence of a substantial and pervasive market failure. Pursuant to its policy statement, CompTIA has written and spoken frequently on antitrust issues of relevance to the technology sector. In June 1998, CompTIA filed an *amicus* brief in the *Intel v. Intergraph* litigation in the U.S. Court of Appeals for the Federal Circuit. In that case CompTIA urged the court to reject a lower court's finding that antitrust allegations could be a basis for ordering a company to disclose its valuable intellectual property.

CompTIA filed an amicus brief in the United States Court of Appeals for the District of Columbia Circuit in the *United States v. Microsoft* case in November 2000. The *amicus* brief urged the Court of Appeals to reverse the District Court's order breaking Microsoft into two separate companies and further urged the Court of Appeals to reverse the liability findings against Microsoft. The basis for CompTIA's participation as *amicus* and submission of this testimony to the Committee is its interest in the overall health and prosperity of the technology sector.

The antitrust case against Microsoft and the final remedies that will be imposed upon Microsoft have a direct effect on the overall health and prosperity of the technology sector. First, because Microsoft is such a large and important participant in the technology industry, any remedy that affects the company's operations necessarily affects the industry, Microsoft's vendors, and all companies that rely on Microsoft products. A remedial order that goes beyond the issues in the case may have a significantly detrimental effect upon innovation and growth in the industry. Second, the precedent established in this case has important ramifications for future activities in the technology sector. Overly restrictive sanctions imposed upon Microsoft may act to inhibit competitive behavior by other companies throughout the industry thereby deterring conduct that promotes innovation and technological development.

INTRODUCTION

On November 6, 2001 the United States Department of Justice and nine States entered into a Proposed Final Judgment with the Microsoft Corporation that resolves the antitrust charges brought by those governmental entities against the company. In the days after the settlement was announced, the nine non-settling States and the District of Columbia expressed their intention to continue litigation against Microsoft in an effort to convince the United States District Court that more extensive remedies should be ordered. On December 7, 2001 the non-settling States filed their remedy proposal with the District Court.

This testimony analyzes the Court of Appeals opinion, the November 6, 2001 Proposed Final Judgment, and the non-settling States' remedy proposal and arrives at the following conclusions:

- The U.S. Court of Appeals June 28, 2001 opinion reaffirmed that the central goal of the U.S. antitrust laws is **not** to protect competitors from competition nor is it to penalize a defendant. The central goal of the antitrust laws is to promote competition in order to enhance consumer welfare.
- In order to support its remedy in the remand proceeding now before the District Court, the Court of Appeals opinion requires that the government show a significant causal connection between Microsoft's anticompetitive conduct and actual injury to competition and consumers in the marketplace. If the government fails to prove a causal connection, then the remedy imposed can be no more broad than an order enjoining the specific anticompetitive conduct at issue.
- Given the risks to both sides from further litigation, the November 6 Proposed Final Judgment is a reasonable settlement of the remaining disputed issues in the case that insures that Microsoft's anticompetitive conduct will not be repeated, and insures that every market participant has a fair opportunity to compete. The settlement also insures that the technology industry will not be encumbered with excessive regulation that would stifle innovation and growth.
- The additional remedies proposed by the non-settling States on December 7 are not likely to enhance competition or promote consumer welfare. The vast majority of the States' proposals go far beyond the scope of the liability found by the Court of Appeals and are thus legally unsupportable. Further, the proposed remedies would likely interfere with natural market forces, impose higher costs on consumers, impair innovation, and benefit Microsoft's competitors at the expense of consumers.

I. SUMMARY OF THE COURT OF APPEALS OPINION

A. Background

On June 28, 2001 the United State Court of Appeals for the District of Columbia Circuit ("Court of Appeals") issued its ruling in *United States v. Microsoft*. The Court of Appeals found that Microsoft had violated Section 2 of the Sherman Act by taking anticompetitive actions to protect its monopoly in the computer operating system market. The Court, however, reversed the District Court rulings entered adverse to Microsoft regarding tying, attempted monopolization, and imposition of a break-up remedy. The case has been remanded to the District Court for proceedings on the appropriate remedy to address the monopoly maintenance findings.

While much of the Court of Appeal's opinion focuses on issues that are specific to Microsoft, the Court made two preliminary yet important observations with respect to antitrust enforcement activities in the high-tech sector. First, the Court noted that despite the relatively fast pace of the Microsoft proceedings, the speed at which technologically dynamic markets undergo change is even faster. The consequences of the speed at which the market changes has significant implications for the conduct of antitrust cases. This rapid change "threatens enormous practical difficulties for courts considering the appropriate measure of relief in equitable enforcement actions, both in crafting injunctive remedies in the first instance and reviewing those remedies in the second." Opinion at 10–11.

Because technology moves so quickly there is little likelihood that a company with large market share at any given time can engage in anticompetitive exclusionary behavior that causes consumer injury. In many instances a more desirable successor technology may very rapidly displace a large market share company before that company is even able to attempt to exercise monopoly power.

Second, the Court also noted that competition in the technology marketplace is frequently "competition for the market" rather than "competition in the market." This means that there is intense competition between firms when a new product is introduced, but once consumers choose the firm that makes the best product, that firm will likely garner the vast majority of market share. This "network effect" phenomenon means that as more users utilize a compatible and inter-operable system or service, the value to each user increases. Opinion at 11–12. Thus, the Court of Appeals made clear that lawful monopolies and companies with large market shares are frequently desirable and highly beneficial to consumers. Opinion at 11.

The Court of Appeal's inclusion of this theoretical discussion is a broad response to the question that many have asked since the beginning of the Microsoft case—that is, do the antitrust laws, written and applied predominantly in a brick-and-mortar era, have the same level of relevance in the information technology era? The answer is mixed. The antitrust laws do apply to the new economy, but the application of the rules must take into account economic realities and to insure that the objectives of antitrust are achieved: the protection and enhancement of competition as measured by consumer welfare.

The most dramatic illustration of the application of antitrust to the new economy was in the Court's rulings on the tying claim and in reversing the lower court's remedial order. The Court's application of a rule of reason analysis (rather than *per se* treatment) for tying claims while at the same time rejecting the "separate products" test marks a significant recognition that product integration in the technology sector is likely to have benefits to consumers that outweigh any harms to competition. Additionally, the Court's analysis in rejecting the lower court's break-up order suggests that absent a strong showing of a causal connection between anticompetitive acts and Microsoft's dominant position in the operating system market, radical structural relief or extensive conduct restrictions that go beyond the challenged conduct would be unsupportable.

B. Monopoly Maintenance

The Court of Appeals affirmed in large measure the District Court's ruling that Microsoft acted unlawfully to maintain its monopoly in the operating system market. The Court found that Microsoft viewed Netscape Navigator Internet browser as a potential threat to the Windows operating system because it could conceivably have become an intermediate platform (with exposed application programming interfaces or API's) for the development of software applications. In order to promote Internet Explorer and retard the distribution of Netscape Navigator, Microsoft placed restrictions on original equipment manufacturers (OEM's). OEM's were not permitted to remove the Internet Explorer icon or install a Navigator icon on the desktop.

The Court also found that the way in which Internet Explorer was integrated into Windows was unlawful. Beginning with the release of Windows 98, Microsoft removed Internet Explorer from the list of programs that could be accessed using in the add/delete program feature. The Court found that this had the effect of impeding the inclusion of rival browsers on a computer because OEM's were reluctant to place two Internet browsers on the desktop. Because Microsoft did not offer any procompetitive justification for preventing the removal of Internet Explorer, the Court found this feature unlawful. The Court also found that Microsoft's dealings with some independent software vendors, Apple Computer Corp., Java, and Intel were designed solely to protect its operating system monopoly and therefore those dealings violated Section 2 of the Sherman Act.

Shortly after the Court of Appeals decision was released, Microsoft announced that it would modify its release of Windows XP to respond to the Court of Appeals rulings in the monopoly maintenance section of the opinion. Thus, OEM's now are permitted to have more control over the appearance of the Windows desktop; they may add icons for competing software and on-line services and delete the Internet Explorer icon from the desktop. OEM's and consumers also have the ability to remove Internet Explorer icon from a computer using the add/delete function.[1]

C. Attempted Monopolization

The Court of Appeals reversed and dismissed the District Court's finding that Microsoft unlawfully attempted to monopolize the Internet browser market. Opinion at 62–68. The District Court had found that Microsoft's 1995 proposal to divide the browser market with Netscape created a dangerous probability of monopoly and that Microsoft's aggressive marketing of Internet Explorer after June 1995 also created a dangerous probability of monopoly. But the Court of Appeals found that the government had failed to properly identify the relevant market including reasonable substitutes for Internet browsers. Further, the Court also found that there was no showing of significant barriers to entry in any putative browser market.

[1] Shortly after the Court of Appeals issued its ruling, Microsoft asked the court to reconsider the finding that Microsoft had unlawfully "commingled" code from Internet Explorer and Windows. Microsoft argued that as a factual matter the District Court was incorrect in finding that Microsoft actually had placed Windows code and Internet Explorer code in the same libraries in order to prevent IE from being removed. The Court of Appeals denied Microsoft's petition for rehearing on this issue but wrote that Microsoft could raise this issue on remand with respect to the appropriate remedy in the case. Microsoft's actions in allowing OEM's and/or consumers to remove the Internet Explorer icon and program link (and the inclusion of that concession in the settlement agreement) appears to address the Court's concerns regarding exclusion of rival browsers. Thus, any interpretation of the Court of Appeals decision to require that Microsoft re-engineer Windows to duplicate shared code functions and then remove the IE code (as the non-settling States interpretation does) would be inconsistent with the language and policy of the opinion as a whole. Further, the Court of Appeals found that shared library files that perform functions for both the operating system and the browser enhance efficiency. Opinion at 73.

The Court's ruling on attempted monopolization has significant implications for future business activities in the technology sector. If the District Court rule had been upheld, the resulting rule would have made it virtually *per se* unlawful for successful firms to explore collaborative relationships with emerging competitors. Further, it would permit a "dangerous probability of success" to be proven simply by showing that a firm has secured a 50–60 percent market share without requiring any showing that the firm will ever be in a position to exercise market power—that is, the power to raise price and exclude competitors. Both propositions would have had serious adverse repercussions for the IT industry and would have likely blocked countless pro-competitive competitor collaborations that would benefit consumers.

D. Tying

The District Court found that Microsoft's inclusion of Internet Explorer with Windows was a *per se* unlawful tying arrangement. The Court of Appeals reversed this conclusion and ruled that *per se* analysis was inappropriate for arrangements involving platform software products. Because the inclusion of added functionality into software products has the potential to be pro-competitive and generate vast consumer benefits, integration in this area must be judged under the rule of reason. The Court of Appeals remanded the tying claim to the District Court for analysis under the rule of reason. Opinion at 68–90. Under the rule of reason, however, future antitrust plaintiffs must bear a heavy burden to prove that software integration unlawful.

Historically tying arrangements have been deemed *per se* unlawful. But the Court properly recognized that software products are "novel categories of dealings" and that this case provided the "first up-close look at the technological integration of added functionality into software that serves as a platform for third-party applications. There being no close parallel in prior antitrust cases, simplistic application of per se tying rules carries a serious risk of harm." Opinion at 69. The Court also noted the benefits from software integration: "Bundling obviously saves distribution and consumer transaction costs." Opinion at 73.

In recognizing the potential benefits from integration, the Court then determined that the "separate products" test under *Jefferson Parish Hosp. Dist. No. 2 v. Hyde*, 466 U.S. 2 (1984)—that is, if the tying and tied products are "separate products" then the integration is unlawful—was not appropriate for platform software analysis.

Finally, the Court of Appeals issued precise instructions to the District Court in considering the tying in the event the government were to pursue the claim on remand. Those instructions preclude the plaintiffs from arguing any theory of anticompetitive harm based on a precise definition of the browser market or barriers to entry in the putative browser market. Opinion at 87. Faced with this new legal standard, the United States, on September 6, 2001, announced that it would not pursue the tying claim on remand.

In sum, adding new functions to existing software is a nearly universal form of innovation in the software industry and is essential in persuading customers to upgrade from their existing software to a new, improved version. For example, word processing programs have incorporated formerly separate spell-checkers and outliners, personal finance programs have incorporated tax functions, internet service providers have incorporated instant messaging features, database software companies are integrating their databases with their applications server, and e-mail programs have incorporated contact managers. If companies that gain a "dominant" position in a given field were barred from innovating in this manner, consumers would be denied new benefits that result from integration, and the software industry would stagnate. The Court of Appeals rejection of a *per se* rule for platform software integration, and the government's subsequent decision to drop that claim on remand, insures that technological innovation will be permitted to continue and provide consumers additional benefits.

E. Remedy

The Court of Appeals fundamentally altered the basis of liability found by the District Court and thus the structural and conduct remedies imposed by the lower court were reversed. Opinion at 106. The Court of Appeals correctly noted that an antitrust remedy must focus on restoring competition and the District Court must explain how its remedy will do so. Opinion at 99–100. Central to the inquiry of how to restore competition is the identification of specific injury to the competitive process by the defendant's behavior. Thus, the Court of Appeals directed the District Court on remand to make a finding of a "causal connection" when assessing an appropriate remedy. Opinion at 105.

While the Court of Appeals left the District Court with a large measure of discretion in fashioning an appropriate remedy on remand, there are repeated and clear directions that the evidence necessary to sustain a structural remedy or extensive conduct remedy must be very strong. Opinion at 105–06. Faced with this language, the United States announced on September 6, 2001 that it would no longer seek break up of Microsoft. The individual States have also dropped their demand for a structural remedy.

The remaining issue for the new District Court judge on remand, Colleen Kollar-Kotelly, is to fashion an appropriate remedy for the monopoly maintenance findings that were affirmed by the Court of Appeals. Here too the Court of Appeals has provided some general guidance. The appropriate remedy for Microsoft's antitrust violations may be "an injunction against continuation of that conduct." Opinion at 105. The language cited by the non-settling States that the unlawful monopoly "must be terminated" would only apply in the context of a demand for structural relief. The non-settling States have not made a demand for structural relief, nor have they made a showing of a causal connection between Microsoft's unlawful behavior and actual harm in the marketplace.

II. SUMMARY OF THE PROPOSED FINAL JUDGMENT

After the November 6, 2001 Proposed Final Judgment was announced many of Microsoft's competitors complained that the settlement was too lenient. The settlement, however, should not be designed as a wish list for Microsoft's competitors. The settlement should fairly address the areas of liability found by the Court of Appeals. Anything less would encourage Microsoft and other companies to engage in anticompetitive conduct in the future; anything more would inappropriately imperil the technology marketplace, cause harm to consumers, and likely be struck down by the Court of Appeals. Additionally, the settlement necessarily takes into account the fact that the issue of causation has not yet been decided by the Court. In light of the scope of the Court of Appeals decision and the uncertainty facing both sides from further litigation, the November 6 Proposed Final Judgment is a reasonable compromise of the antitrust litigation.

The November 6 Proposed Final Judgment addresses the liability issues in the monopoly maintenance section of the Court of Appeals decision, and correctly does not seek to impose a remedy related to other areas in which Microsoft prevailed on appeal—attempted monopolization and tying.

First, the settlement prohibits Microsoft from retaliating against any OEM because of the OEM's participation in promoting or developing non-Microsoft middleware or a non-Microsoft operating system. This provision takes the "club" out of Microsoft's hand and prevents the company from using anticompetitive means to discourage OEM's from promoting or preventing rival software from being developed or installed on Windows desktop. This anti-retaliation provision deals head on with most of the conduct the Court of Appeals found to be illegal in the monopoly maintenance section of its June 28, 2001 opinion.

Second, Microsoft is obligated to adhere to one uniform license agreement for Windows with all OEM's and the royalty for the license shall be made publicly available on a web site accessible by all OEM's. The price schedule may vary for volume discounts and for those OEM's who are eligible for market development allowances in connection with Windows products. This allows Microsoft to continue to compete in the middleware market with other middleware manufacturers and this competition will continue to benefit consumers.

Third, OEM's are permitted to alter the appearance of the Windows desktop to add icons, shortcuts and menu items for non-Microsoft middleware, and they may establish non-Microsoft programs as default programs in Windows. Consumers also have the option of removing the interface with any Microsoft middleware product.

Fourth, Microsoft must reveal the API's used by Microsoft middleware to interoperate with the Windows operating system. Microsoft must also offer to license its intellectual property rights to any entity who has need for the intellectual property to insure that their products will interoperate with the Windows operating system.

These central features of the settlement insure that other companies have the ability to challenge Microsoft products, both in the operating system and middleware / applications markets. Consumers and OEM's have far greater freedom to install and use non-Microsoft products, Microsoft is prohibited from retaliating against any entity who promotes non-Microsoft programs, and all companies have equal access to Microsoft API's and technical information so that non-Microsoft middleware has the same opportunity to perform as well as Microsoft middleware.

The enforcement mechanisms of the settlement will enable the plaintiffs to insure Microsoft's compliance with the agreement. Representatives of the United States and the States may inspect Microsoft's books, records, source code or any other item to insure compliance with the settlement terms. In addition, an independent three person technical Committee will be established to insure that Microsoft complies with all terms of the settlement agreement. The technical Committee will have full access to all Microsoft source code, books and records, and personnel and can report to the United States and/or the States any violation of the settlement by Microsoft.

III. SUMMARY OF THE NON-SETTLING STATES' DECEMBER 7 PROPOSAL

While the November 6 Proposed Final Judgment goes beyond the liability found by the Court of Appeals in some areas (i.e., by requiring Microsoft to disclose its confidential technical information to software developers), the non-settling States' proposal filed on December 7, 2001 goes so far beyond the judgment as to bear little relationship to the Court of Appeals decision.

The centerpiece of the states' remedy demand is that Microsoft be compelled to create and market a stripped down version of its Windows operating system that would not include many of the features that current versions of Windows do include. Since consumers can now easily remove Microsoft features from their desktop and OEM's are free to place non-Microsoft programs on the desktop, it is difficult to see how this requirement would benefit consumers.

Instead of giving consumers more choices of software products, this unwarranted intrusion into marketing and design decision by the non-settling States would cause further delays in the development of software created to run on XP, with developers waiting to see which version would become the standard. Such delays would further postpone the salutary effects of XP on the computer market. It would also hamper programmers' ability to take full advantage of technological improvements in Windows, creating a marketplace in which the same software applications would not perform equally. This remedy would balkanize the computing industry and would undermine the benefits consumers obtain from a standardized operating platform.

In addition to the stripped down version of Windows, the December 7 proposal would also require Microsoft to continue licensing and supporting prior versions of Windows for five years after the introduction of a new version of Windows. The primary effect of this requirement is to impose unnecessary costs upon Microsoft (that would likely be passed on to consumers) and reduce the incentives for Microsoft to improve the operating system. This disincentive to Microsoft to make technological advances would ripple throughout the software industry as applications developers would not have an advancing platform to write software to.

The non-settling States remedy proposal also includes a variety of restrictions that will have little if any quantifiable benefit to consumers but which will simply advance the interests of Microsoft competitors. Consumers and OEM's currently have full ability and freedom to include Java software on their computers; the States' requirement that Microsoft carry Java on all copies of Windows does not provide consumers or OEM's with any more choice than they already have. Similarly, the requirement that Microsoft continue to produce an Office Suite for Macintosh interferes with natural market forces that direct resources to the best use and may actually preclude the success of competing applications software. Directing Microsoft to produce and support any software without regard for market forces is likely to harm consumers, not help them. Moreover, the November 6 Proposed Judgment fully addresses and prevents Microsoft from retaliating or taking any anticompetitive actions against Apple.

Advances in technology are frequently made as a result of joint ventures between competitors. The Department of Justice and the Federal Trade Commission have recently released guidelines for the formation of such joint ventures. Notwithstanding the recognition by these enforcement agencies that most joint ventures are pro-competitive, the non-settling States seek to restrict Microsoft from entering into joint ventures whereby the parties to the joint venture agree not to compete with the product that is the subject of the joint venture. This restriction will chill innovation and prohibit countless consumer welfare enhancing arrangements. Further, this proposal flatly ignores the fact that the Court of Appeals found in Microsoft's favor on the issue of the alleged illegality of its joint venture proposal to Netscape.

The most harmful of the remaining remedy proposals include those that require the extensive and mandatory sharing of Microsoft's intellectual property. The non-settling States proposals in this regard go well beyond those in the November 6 Proposed Final Judgment and appear to be aimed at benefitting Microsoft's competitors rather than insuring a level playing field for all participants in the software industry. 1n the absence of compelling justification for wholesale and forced disclosure of a company's intellectual property, the harm caused by such disclosure is unwarranted and harmful to the entire technology marketplace. The vigorous protection of intellectual property has fueled the rapid and dynamic growth of the technology industry. Actions that erode protections for intellectual property should be viewed with great trepidation.

The long term effects of the conduct restrictions proposed by the non-settling States encourage continued litigation, rather than competition in the marketplace.

CONCLUSION

The Microsoft settlement and any remedies imposed must be judged in the context of the Court of Appeals opinion. The non-settling States remedial proposals go well beyond the liability found by the Court of Appeals. The Microsoft case, and this Committee hearing, should not be a forum for any government actor, no matter how well-intentioned, to try to reconfigure the marketplace based on guesswork and supposition. History has told us time and time again that government's efforts to micromanage markets are far more likely to fail than to succeed. Consumers stand to lose the most.

The Plaintiffs have never challenged Microsoft's acquisition of its dominant position in the operating system market. Microsoft was propelled into this position as a result of consumer choice. Consumers derive great benefit from the adoption of a standardized operating system platform. State antitrust officials and the courts should be wary of imposing remedies that would interfere with the positive network effects resulting from the large number of consumers who choose Windows.

Government intervention in the marketplace can only be justified if the intervention is a reasonably accurate proxy for the actions that would occur in a competitive market. Otherwise, the unintended consequences of well-meaning government intervention are very likely to do more harm than good. It is simply beyond the capability of the courts and regulators to predict the direction and development of almost any market, let alone the highly dynamic markets in the technology industry. This counsels against the extensive and rigid conduct restrictions proposed by the non-settling States.

Statement of Dr. Mark N. Cooper, Director of Research, Consumer Federation of America, Washington, D.C.

Mr. Chairman and Members of the Committee,

My name is Dr. Mark Cooper. I am Director of Research of the Consumer Federation of America. The Consumer Federation of America is the nation's largest consumer advocacy group, composed of two hundred and seventy state and local affiliates representing consumer, senior citizen. low-income, labor, farm, public power, and cooperative organizations, with more than fifty million individual members.

I greatly appreciate the opportunity to appear before you today. This hearing on "The Microsoft Settlement: A Look To the Future" focuses public policy attention on exactly the right questions. What should the software market look like? Does the Court of Appeals' ruling provide an adequate legal foundation for creating that market? Is it worth the effort? What specific remedies are necessary to get the job done?

Our analysis of the Microsoft case over four years leads us to clear answers.[1]

- We reject the claim that consumers must accept monopoly in the software industry. Real competition can work in the software market, but it will never get a chance if Microsoft is not forced to abandon the pervasive pattern of anticompetitive practices it has used to dominate product line after product line.
- The antitrust case has revealed a massive violation of the antitrust laws. A unanimous decision of the Appeals Court points the way to restoring competition.
- The public interest demands that we try.
- The proposed Microsoft-Department of Justice settlement is far too weak to accomplish that goal. The litigating states' remedial proposals are now the only

[1] *The Consumer Case Against Microsoft* (October 1998); *The Consumer Cost of the Microsoft Monopoly: $10 Billion and Counting* (January 1999); *Economic Evidence in the Antitrust Trial: The Microsoft Defense Stumbles Over the Facts* (March 18, 1999); *Facts Law and Antitrust Remedies: Time for Microsoft to be Held Accountable for its Monopoly Abuses* (May 2000) (Attachment A); Mark Cooper, "Antitrust as Consumer Protection in the New Economy: Lessons from the Microsoft Case," *Hasting Law Journal*, 52 (April 2001) (see Attachment B); *Windows XP/.NET: Microsoft's Expanding Monopoly, How it Can Harm Consumers and What the Courts Must Do to Preserve Competition* (September 26, 2001) (see Attachment C).

chance that consumers have of enjoying the benefits of competition in the industry.

Real Competition In The Software Industry Is The Goal

The defenders of the Microsoft monopoly say that consumers cannot hope for competition within software markets because this is a winner-take-all, new economy industry. In this product space companies always win the whole market or most of it, so anything goes. In fact. Microsoft's expert witness has written in a scholarly journal that:

> With "winner take most" markets. . . [If] there can be only one healthy survivor, the incumbent market leader must exclude its competition or die. . . There is no useful nonexclusion baseline, which the traditional test for predation requires. . .
>
> As to intent, in a struggle for survival that will have only one winner, any firm must exclude rivals to survive. . . . In a winner take most market, evidence that A intends to kill B merely confirms A's desire to survive.[2]

By that standard, if a monopolist burned down the facilities of a potential competitor, it might be guilty of arson and other civil crimes, but it would not be guilty of violating the antitrust laws. Consumers should be thankful that both the trial court and the Appeals Court flatly rejected this theory of the inevitability of monopoly and upheld the century old standard of competition.

In fact, the products against which Microsoft has directed its most violent anticompetitive attacks represent the best form of traditional competition—compatible products that operate on top of existing platforms seeking to gain market share by enhancing functionality and expanding consumer choice.[3] Microsoft fears these products and seeks to destroy them, not compete against them, precisely because they represent uncontrolled compatibility, rampant interoperability and, over the long-term, potential alternatives to the Windows operating system.

That is why we concluded over three years ago that this case is not about new high tech industries in which you have to live with a monopoly, it is about old dirty business practices that drive up prices, deny consumers choice and slow innovation by allowing the monopolist to control the pace of product development.[4] If a monopoly were really the natural state of affairs in this market, then Microsoft would not have had to engage in so many unnatural acts to preserve it.

More importantly. we concluded that consumers need not fear real competition in the software industry. We can expect a competitive market to be far more efficient and consumer friendly than the Microsoft monopoly. There are a variety of very real consumer costs associated with the Windows operating system monopoly—from product complexity and PC homogeneity to viruses, privacy threats and an endless cycle of costly upgrades—even apart from the substantial overcharges Microsoft has for years imposed on consumers. There is every reason to believe that consumers would receive better products at lower prices if the anticompetitive practices were eliminated. The ability of developers to create products that are compatible, but driven out of the market by Microsoft's anticompetitive tactics, undermines the claim and lays to rest any fears that competition will cause computing to become more difficult or confusing.

An Effective Remedy is Fully Supported and is Required by the Trial Record

The claim by Microsoft and others that the court record will not support a strong remedy is simply wrong. The Court of Appeals not only reaffirmed our belief in real competition, but it pointed the way to competition by using the strongest terms possible to describe what the remedy must do.

> The Supreme Court has explained that a remedies decree in an antitrust case must seek to 'unfetter a market from anticompetitive conduct,' *Ford Motor Co.*, 405 U.S. at 577, to 'terminate the illegal monopoly, deny to the defendant the fruits of its statutory violation, and ensure that there remain no practices likely to result in monopolization in the future,' *United States v. United Shoe Mach. Corp.*, 391 U.S. 244, 250 (1968): *see also United States v. Grinnell Corp.*, 384 U.S. 563, 577 (1966).[5]

A unanimous *en banc* Court of Appeals upheld the charge of monopolization. It explicitly affirmed Microsoft's liability under Section 2 of the Sherman Act, the vast

---

[2] Richard Schmalensee, "Antitrust Issues in Schumpeterian Industries," *90 American Economic Review* 192–194 (2000).

[3] Mark Cooper, *Antitrust and Consumer Protection*, pp. 863–880.

[4] *The Consumer Case Against Microsoft*, pp. 53–59.

[5] *U.S. v. Microsoft*, 253 F.3d 34, 103 (D.C. Cir. 2001) (*en banc*).

bulk of the specific conduct challenged by the Department of Justice, *and nearly every one of the trial court's hundreds of factual findings*. As a result, it held a broad array of anticompetitive Microsoft practices to be illegal, constituting a massive violation of the antitrust law. Table 1 identifies those anticompetitive practices that were directly linked to the violations of law.

Soon after the district court's Conclusions of Law were released, we considered possible remedies.[6] While we preferred a break up, we also identified a series of conduct remedies that would address the anticompetitive problems. The litigating states have risen to the task admirably. As described in Table 2, the litigating states' remedial proposals link each relief measure directly to a finding of fact and a conclusion of law. They included virtually every measure we deemed necessary.

An Effective Remedy is Well Worth Fighting For

Based on the record of the lower court and the ruling of the D.C. Circuit, this case demands a strong remedy. Claims that a weak remedy sooner is better than a strong remedy later, or that the cost of pursuing a strong remedy are too great, are absurd.

Our analysis leads us to conclude that an unfettered software market will produce a flowering of innovations and consumer-friendly products that are well worth waiting for. More importantly, we have estimated that monopoly pricing by Microsoft has cost consumers between $10 and $20 billion.[7] An *amicus* brief filed with the court put the figure at $25 to $30 billion.

Of equal importance are the non-economic and indirect ways in which Microsoft's anticompetitive practices become burdens on the consumer. The trial record demonstrates. with extensive evidence. repeated instances in which Microsoft's anticompetitive practices have the effect of denying consumers choice, impairing quality, and slowing innovation.

Microsoft forces computer manufacturers to buy one bundle with all of its programs preloaded. It biases the screen location. start sequences and default options making it difficult if not impossible to choose non-Microsoft products. Products tailored to meet individual consumer needs (consumer friendly configurations and small bundles) are unavailable. Because of Microsoft's leveraging of the operating system, superior products are delayed or driven from the marketplace. Existing libraries of content (documents, movies, audio files) are rendered obsolete. Resources are denied, investment in competing products is chilled, and technology is slowed. Valuable products never get to market because of the barriers erected by Microsoft and eventually competing products disappear from the market.

Past overcharges cannot be recovered in the Federal case nor can innovations that were slowed or stopped, but future abuse must be prevented. We are convinced that an effective remedy will trigger an explosion of innovation and economic activity from thousands of companies that have been shackled by the fear of retribution or expropriation by Microsoft. Unleashing these companies to innovate in a vigorously competitive market is the best way to stimulate economic activity and to put this industry on a solid long-term growth path. Settling for a short term fix, in the name of economic stimulus, that fails to address the underlying problem will create a chronic condition of underperformance, leaving the industry far short of achieving it true potential.

We are also certain that the Microsoft-DOJ settlement will not do the job but make matters worse. Our review of Windows XP, from a competitive point of view, confirms our conclusion from four years ago that "the threat to the public has grown with each subsequent conquest of a market."[8]

There is no doubt that effective law enforcement is definitely in the consumer's best interest and that the Microsoft-Department of Justice settlement is not. Based on the legal record, the weakness of the remedy, and the stakes for consumers, the court must find that the proposed Microsoft-Department of Justice settlement is not in the public interest. The court should certainly not reach any conclusion about the remedy that would best serve the public before the litigating states' remedial proposal has been fully vetted through the trial process.

Anticompetitive Practices Must Be Rooted Out At All Stages Of the Software Value Chain—Creation, Distribution And Use

To describe what must be done in practical terms, I like to use the business school concept of the value chain. To unfetter the market from anticompetitive conduct,

[6] *Facts, Law and Remedies*
[7] Cooper, *Antitrust as Consumer Protection*, pp. 840–862.
[8] *The Consumer Case Against Microsoft*, p. 54, see also pp. 34–39 for a discussion of Microsoft's attack on the Internet, a theme that is picked up in *Windows XP/.NET*.

terminate the illegal monopoly and ensure that there remain no practices likely to result in monopolization in the future, the remedy must address the creation, distribution and use of software. In order for new software to have a fair chance to compete the remedy must

- create an environment in which independent software vendors and alternative platform developers are free to develop products that compete with Windows and with other Microsoft products,
- free computer manufacturers to install these products without fear of retaliation, and
- enable consumers to choose among them with equal ease as with Microsoft products.

The Microsoft-Department of Justice settlement is an abysmal failure at all three levels. Under the proposed Microsoft-Department of Justice settlement, Microsoft will be undeterred from continuing its anticompetitive business practices.

Independent software vendors and competing platform developers will get little relief from Microsoft's continual practice of hiding and manipulating interfaces. Microsoft has the unreviewable ability under the proposed settlement to define Windows itself, and. therefore to control whether and how independent software developers will be able to write programs that run on top of the operating system. The definitions of software products and functionalities and the decisions about how to configure applications programming interfaces are left in the hands of Microsoft to such an extent that it will be encouraged to embed the critical technical specifications deeply into the operating system and thereby prevent independent software developers from seeing them. To the extent that Microsoft would actually be required to reveal anything, it would be so late in the product development cycle that independent software developers would never be able to catch up to Microsoft's favored developers. Furthermore, the Court of Appeals recognized that the Microsoft monopoly is protected by a large barrier to entry, because many crucial applications are available only for Windows. The proposed settlement does nothing to undermine this "applications barrier to entry," for instance by requiring the porting of Microsoft Office to other PC platforms. Thus, the DOJ proposal won't restore competition; it all but legalizes Microsoft's previous anticompetitive strategy and, in reality, institutionalizes the Windows monopoly

Computer manufacturers will not be shielded from retaliation by Microsoft. The restriction on retaliation against computer manufacturers leaves so many loopholes that any OEM who actually went against Microsoft's wishes would be committing commercial suicide. Microsoft is given free reign to favor some, at the expense of others through incentives and joint ventures. It is free to withhold access to its other two monopolies (the browser and Office) as an inducement to favor the applications that Microsoft is targeting at new markets, which invites a repeat of the fiasco in the browser wars. Retaliation in any way, shape, fit, form, or fashion should be illegal. The prohibition on retaliation must specifically identify price and non-price discrimination and apply to all monopoly products.

Consumer sovereignty is not restored by the settlement. Because the settlement does not require removal of applications, only the hiding of icons, Microsoft preserves the ability to neuter consumer choice. The boot screen and desktop remain entirely tilted against competition. Microsoft still is allowed to be the pervasive default option and allowed to harass consumers who switch to non-Microsoft applications and still gets to sweep those applications off the desktop, forcing consumers to choose them over and over.

Given Microsoft's Past Behavior, Enforcement Must Be Swift and Punishment for non-Compliance Must be Substantial

After the court identifies remedies that can address these problems, it must enforce them swiftly and aggressively. Microsoft has shown through a decade of investigations, consent decrees and litigation that it will not be easily deterred from defending and extending its monopoly. It behaves as though it believes its expert witness and has the right to do whatever it wants to kills off its competition. Every one of the illegal acts that led to the District Court findings and the unanimous appeals court ruling of liability took place after Microsoft signed the last consent decree.

With three monopolies to use against its potential competitors (the Windows operating system, the Internet Explorer browser, and Office in desktop applications), enforcement must be swift and sure, or competition will never have a chance to take root. The proposed settlement offers virtually nothing in this regard. The technical Committee that is set up to (maybe) hear complaints can be easily tied up in knots by Microsoft because of the vague language of the settlement. If Microsoft violates the settlement nothing happens to the company, except that it must "endure" the annoyance of putting up with this weak settlement for a couple more years.

The Future of Effective Antitrust Demands A Strong Remedy

I pointed out several months before the Court of Appeals ruled that we fully support a rule of reason for tying in the software industry. as long as the rules are reasonable.[9] The Microsoft-Department of Justice settlement is not worthy of the thoughtful ruling of the Court of Appeals. Indeed, this Committee should be deeply troubled by the proposed settlement. By proposing such a weak remedy for such a strong case and well-articulated ruling, it could do permanent damage to the antitrust laws. 'shy bother to bring a case if law enforcement is going to drop the ball at the last moment?

The Consumer Federation of America is procompetitive when it comes to market structure and generally argues for a rule of reason based on fundamentals of economic cost-benefits analysis. However, good consumer economic analysis demands that the rule of reason be based on reasonable rules. The analytic framework must be able to comprehend basic empirical facts in a manner that coherently and realistically integrates economic structure, conduct and performance. There should be no presumptions in favor of, or against business. The discount rate should reflect the real rate of interest that consumers can earn. The value of a person's time and risk of harm should reflect the economic and intrinsic value of life. The Microsoft case rewards this pragmatic approach to policy analysis handsomely.

I greatly appreciate the opportunity to appear before you today. I look forward to coming back after the trial court hands down a serious remedy based on the proposal laid before it by the litigating Attorneys General. I am confident that the court will reject the Microsoft-Department of Justice settlement because it does not do justice to competition, consumers or the clear and insightful conclusions of the Court of Appeals Court—in short it is not in the public interest.

[9] *Id.*, p. 1.

TABLE 1
ABUSIVE BUSINESS PRACTICES IDENTIFIED IN THE FINDINGS OF FACT AND CONCLUSIONS OF LAW UPHELD BY THE APPEALS COURT

ANTICOMPETITIVE CONDITIONS/PRACTICES	FINDINGS OF FACT (Paragraph No.)	CONCLUSIONS OF LAW (Page No.)	LITIGATING STATES' REMEDIAL PROPOSALS (Paragraph No.)
Monopoly Position	18-21,33-35	4,5	
Barriers To Entry			
Hardware	19,22-27, 54-55	4,6	4
Software	30,36-43,141,166	4,5,6	14
Abrogation Of Contracts	390,394	18	
Intimidation	106,129,236,355	6,10	15, 20
Market Division	88,105	10,22	11
Bounty	139,260,295	16,20	11
Predation	107, 147	6,10,16,21,22	1
Bundling			
Os Tying	159, 170,198	4,11,12,31	12, 13
Imitation	133-134,166	10,18,19,22	11
Contract Provisions			
Exclusive Deals	143,147,230-234,247 259-260,287-290,293-297 305-306,317-321 326-326,332,337 339-340,350-352	10,15,37,38	6, 7
Preferred Desktop Location	139,272,301	17,20	2, 10
Secret Price	64,118,236-238,324	6,10,11	1
Indirect Sales	10,19,103	4,6,10	
Quality Impairment	90-92,128-129,160, 330,339-340	6,11	4
Resource Denial	240,357,379,396-406	31	8, 9
Disabling	160,170-172	11,31,32	4, 5
Desupporting	90,122,128-129, 192,405-406	10,18	3. 16
Deny Consumers User-Friendly	210-216	11	2, 10
Thwart Responses to Consumer Demand	225-229	11,14	2, 10
Impair the Functionality of Non-Microsoft Products	92,128-129, 160,171-172, 330,339,340	6,10,11,17,32	4, 5

TABLE 2
CONDUCT REMEDIES FOR PRACTICES THAT VIOLATE LAW

PRACTICE	REMEDY	LITIGATING STATES' REMEDIAL PROPOSALS
UNDER THE TABLE	Liability Under Law	1, 11, 15, 20
APPLICATIONS BARRIER TO ENTRY	Port office to competing OS	14
	Remedy applies to "Windows Family" Applications Distribution channels ISVs	1, 3
CONTRACT		
Exclusive/Preferential	Ban exclusives	6
	Prohibition on discrimination Price Functionality Support Testing Marketing Other "inducements"	2, 7
	Ban NDAs	15
Indirect Sales/Hidden Price	Transparent prices	2
QUALITY IMPAIRMENT		
Resource Denial	Prohibition on discrimination	2
Incompatibility/Integration	Access to source code	4, 5
Disabling	API disclosure	4, 5
	Neutral warning message	
Desupporting	Support older OS	3, 16
	Provide training	4
BUNDLING		
OS Tying	Spin off browser	12, 13
Imitation	Separate sale requirement	1
PRICE ABUSE		
Discrimination/Secret Price	Transparent prices	1, 2
Cross-subsidy/Predation	Transparent prices, separate sale	1, 2
Upgrade Policy	Restrict old OS price increase	
	Backward compatibility	
Excessive functionality	Support older OS versions	3
	Backward compatibility	3
CONSUMER HARM		
Impairing Non-Microsoft Thwarting Responses	API disclosure,	4
	Boot screen, start sequence freedom	2, 10
Forcing Inefficient Acquisition	Ban exclusives	6
	Prohibition on discrimination	8, 9

Statement of Mark Havlicek, Digital Data Resources, Inc., Des Moines, Iowa

Thank you, Chairman Leahy and distinguished Members of the Committee including my own Senator Grassley. I am pleased to contribute my comments to your hearing on "The Microsoft Settlement: A Look to the Future." My name is Mark Havlicek and I am the President of Digital Data Resources, Inc. in Des Moines, Iowa. I have been actively involved in the technology industry for several years, and it is my hope that the Microsoft case will be settled.

The economic outlook for 2002 is very concerning. From coast to coast, revenue growth has slowed, spending is exceeding budgeted levels, and many states are looking at large budget cuts. My own state of Iowa is in the middle of a terrible budget crisis.

After the events of September 11, we saw a dramatic plunge in the technology sector. Instead of being tied up in court, technology entrepreneurs should at work developing products and charting new territory with never before imagined products and services. Given the opportunity and free of unnecessary hurdles to progress, technology companies can build our economy back up to record levels.

Giants like Apple, IBM, and Microsoft provide a stable environment for the myriad small firms, like mine, to create, develop, and release new cutting-edge technologies and employ additional people in good paying careers. Small companies like my own, work in concert, and competition at times, with these giants. This mutually dependent relationship is the lifeblood of our industry and a driving force behind our growth.

Over the past 20 years, we have seen computers go from the size of a refrigerator to the size of a deck of cards. And in tandem with those leaps forward, we have seen declining prices, better and faster technology, and increasingly more efficient methods of delivery to consumers.

It takes a competitive, entrepreneurial spirit to survive in this exceptionally aggressive industry of ours, especially in the case of small or emerging businesses. We spend our days watching competitors, finding markets, and keeping a watchful eye on the economy. And it seemed the storm has passed, both figuratively and in the eyes of the stock market, when a settlement was announced last month.

But the states, including my own state of Iowa, which remain involved have argued for tougher enforcement provisions, including a court-appointed "special master" to oversee Microsoft's compliance. And we have found through experience that there is no remedy discrete to Microsoft when it's the nucleus of a tech sector that operates as its own economy.

These states are not right to push ahead for further prosecution of Microsoft. The proposed settlement is sufficient to address the concerns of business people like me who are in the technology industry and are most affected. Companies like mine strive to be similar to Microsoft and we are discouraged by the hold-out states position on further action. *It seems to me to be a strong disincentive to progress and entrepreneurial achievement.*

The time to take a hard line on successful companies like Microsoft is over. The hold-out states are holding out to the detriment of their state economies and our national economy at a time when actions like this are not at all useful.

It is a frightening prospect to see another dollar of precious development resources diverted to paying attorney's fees instead of rippling through our industry. Money that could have launched a new product or created new opportunities for a small business on the brink instead has disappeared into the abyss of this lawsuit. The settlement is a positive step in putting it all behind us and opening a new chapter in the life of the technology industry.

I applaud Assistant Attorney General Charles James for his role in bringing the case this far. The settlement agreement is a strong one. It will have an enormous, positive impact on the future of my company and the entire software industry. My colleagues and I hope we can rely on your support. Thank you, Senators, for the opportunity to provide this statement at such a critical for our nation.

Thank You.

Statement of Dave Baker, Vice President for Law and Public Policy EarthLink Inc., Atlanta, Georgia

My name is Dave Baker and I am Vice President for Law and Public Policy with EarthLink. EarthLink is the nation's 3rd largest Internet Service Provider, bringing reliable high-speed internet connections to approximately 4.8 million subscribers every day. Headquartered in Atlanta, EarthLink provides a full range of innovative access, hosting and e-commerce solutions to thousands of communities over a nationwide network of dial-up points of presence, as well as high-speed access and wireless technologies.

EarthLink is concerned with the potential for Microsoft to use its affirmed monopoly position in operating systems to leverage its position in innovative Internet services provided by Internet Service Providers (ISPs) including Internet access and associated services.

The proposed Justice Department settlement with Microsoft allows them to continue to restrict competition and choice in ISP services by failing to classify e-mail client software and Internet access software as "middleware". By not including e-mail client and internet access software in the definition of middleware, this proposed settlement allows Microsoft to force OEMs to carry Microsoft's own ISP service, Microsoft Network (MSN), while restricting them from carrying competing e-mail client software or internet access software. The federal settlement also allows Microsoft to prohibit OEMs from removing the MSN from their products.

The alternate settlement proposed by nine States and the District of Columbia would define middleware to include e-mail client software and Internet access software, thereby preserving competition in these markets. This distinction in the definition of middleware makes a huge difference given the diverse nature of the ISP marketplace. Many ISPs will never find a place on the Microsoft desktop if Microsoft can prohibit OEMs from including competing e-mail client software and Internet access software, or if Microsoft is able to make such software incompatible with the Windows operating system.

ISPs provide distinct and valuable services beyond mere Internet connectivity. For example, ISPs provide specialized content, web hosting, e-commerce, content specialized for wireless access, and other innovative new products. ISPs provide free local computer and Internet classes for their customers, include local content on their home page, or provide free connections for community groups. EarthLink, while serving a broad range of users across the country, has made greater privacy protection a distinguishing feature of its ISP service. This diverse choice of service and source of future innovation is at risk if Microsoft is able to leverage its existing monopoly power in operating systems to all but force consumers to use its Internet access service, MSN, at the expense of other choices in internet service.

Over the past few years, Microsoft has bundled its internet service more and more closely with succeeding versions of the Windows operating system. This has allowed Microsoft to constrict consumer choice in Internet access providers. In Windows 98, consumers had a choice of several ISPs from which to select for Internet access. Each ISP was listed in the same manner, with equal sized boxes on a referral server screen. In Windows Me, the MSN butterfly icon was the only ISP icon featured right on the desktop, giving it an advantage shared by no other ISP. Consumer had to click down through several screens to find other ISPs. Now, Windows XP has a dialogue boxes that pops up and several times to try to sway consumers to sign up for MSN internet service. While it is possible to select another ISP, this choice is buried and requires greater effort and diligence on the part of the consumer. This illustrates how Microsoft can use its control of the desktop to promote its own Internet access and related content, applications and services.

Under the proposed federal settlement, even this limited choice can be eliminated by Microsoft, since they would be free to restrict OEMs from offering other ISPs on the desktop or from removing Microsoft's own icons from the desktop.

On a related topic, Microsoft recently offered to settle numerous lawsuits by donating computer equipment to schools. Apple Computer has raised concerns that this donation would give Microsoft an inappropriate advantage in gaining greater market share for its operating system in the competitive school marketplace. EarthLink is also concerned that Microsoft would use the proposed computer donations (a good thing) to access with equipment and operating software. This would again unfairly steer consumers, including as here those least able to exercise choice in their internet applications, into using just associated Microsoft products.

We note that the E-Rate, the federal grant program for school connectivity, requires that schools be allowed to purchase Internet access from a range of competitive providers. The government's clear intent is for schools to have a choice of competitive Internet access providers, in order to promote the broadest selection of services, diversity and choice of features, and lowest prices for Internet access. This intent would be undermined if Microsoft uses its proposed computer donations as a "Trojan horse" to install yet more of its own e-mail client and Internet access software. We encourage the preservation of choice for these schools and their students in their selection of Internet access and related services.

EarthLink is concerned that just as Microsoft used its Windows operating system monopoly to force consumers to use the Microsoft browser, Internet Explorer, at the expense of competitors such as Netscape Navigator, Microsoft is now seeking to use the same leverage to force consumers to use their Internet service providers, MSN. EarthLink supports the alternate settlement proposed by the nine States to preserve competition in the market for email client software and Internet access software by including these services in the definition of middleware. As it considers the future of the Internet marketplace, we encourage the Committee not to allow Microsoft to leverage its existing monopoly into new and evolving Internet services. Thank you for giving us the opportunity to share our views with the Committee.

Statement of Jay L. Himes, Chief, Antitrust Bureau, Office of the Attorney General, State of New York, New York, N.Y.

Chairman Leahy and distinguished Members of this Committee, thank you for inviting me to testify before you today on the important issues relating to the settlement of the case against Microsoft, brought by the Antitrust Division of the United States Department of Justice, 18 States and the District of Columbia. New York is one of the lead States in this lawsuit, and we have had a central role in the matter going back to the investigation that led to the filing of the case.

As the members of the Committee know, on Friday, November 2, 2001, the DOJ and Microsoft reached a proposed settlement of the lawsuit, which was then publicly announced. After further negotiations between Microsoft and the States, a revised settlement was reached on Tuesday, November 6, 2001. New York—together with the States of Illinois, Kentucky, Louisiana, Maryland, Michigan, North Carolina, Ohio and Wisconsin—agreed to the revised settlement. The remaining State plaintiffs—California, Connecticut, Florida, Iowa, Kansas, Massachusetts, Minnesota, Utah, West Virginia and the District of Columbia—are seeking a judicially ordered remedy, as is their right.

I, together with an Assistant Attorney General from the State of Ohio, were the principal representatives of the States in the lengthy negotiations that led to the proposed final judgment embodying the settlement. Therefore, I believe that we in New York see the Microsoft settlement from a vantage point that others who were notin the negotiating room may lack. I will do my best to try to share our observations with the Committee. I will begin by presenting an overview of the lawsuit and the settlement reached. After that, I will address in more detail several of the central features of the settlement. Then, I wish to turn to the settlement process itself, particularly insofar as it bears on criticism of the proposed final judgment.

1. Overview of the Case and the Settlement

In May 1998, New York, 18 other States and the District of Columbia began a lawsuit against Microsoft, alleging violations of federal and state antitrust laws.[1] The States' case was similar to an antitrust case commenced that same day by DOJ, and the two cases proceeded on a consolidated basis. In summary, the litigation against Microsoft charged that the company unlawfully restrained trade and denied consumers choice by: (1) monopolizing the market for personal computer ("PC") operating systems; (2) bundling (or "tying") Internet Explorer—Microsoft's web browser—into the Windows operating system used on most PCs; (3) entering into arrangements with various industry members that excluded competitive software; and (4) attempting to monopolize the market for web browsers.

After a lengthy trial, the District Court upheld the governments' claims that Microsoft had unlawfully: (1) maintained a monopoly in the PC operating system market; (2) tied Internet Explorer to its Windows operating system monopoly; and (3) attempted to monopolize the browser market. The District Court issued a final judgment breaking up Microsoft into two separate businesses, and ordering certain conduct remedies intended to govern Microsoft's business activities pending completion of the break-up. These remedies were stayed while Microsoft appealed.

In June of this year, the Court of Appeals for the District of Columbia Circuit issued its decision on appeal. *United States v. Microsoft Corp.*, 253 F.3d 34 (D.C. Cir. 2001). The Court of Appeals broadly upheld the lower court's monopolization maintenance ruling, although it rejected a few of the acts of monopolization found by the District Court including the Court's determination that Microsoft's overall course of conduct itself amounted to monopoly maintenance. On the tying claim, the Court of Appeals reversed the lower court's holding of an antitrust violation, and

[1] Subsequently, one State (South Carolina) dropped out, and another (New Mexico) settled earlier this year.

ordered a new trial under the rule of reason—a standard more favorable to Microsoft than the standard previously used by the trial court. In view of these rulings, the Circuit Court vacated the final judgment, including the break-up provisions. Finally, the Court of Appeals disqualified the trial judge from hearing further proceedings. Thereafter, the Court of Appeals denied a rehearing petition by Microsoft, and the Supreme Court declined to hear an appeal by Microsoft concerning the Court of Appeals' disqualification ruling.

The Court of Appeals returned the case to the District Court in late August of this year. At that point, a new judge—Hon. Colleen Kollar-Kotelly—was assigned. Shortly after that, DOJ and the States announced their intention, in the forthcoming proceedings before the District Court, to refrain from seeking another break up order—and to focus instead on conduct remedies modeled on those included in the earlier District Court judgment. DOJ and the States also announced that they would not retry the tying claim under the rule of reason test that the Court of Appeals had adopted. These decisions by the government enforcers were made in an effort to jump-start the process of promptly obtaining a strong and effective remedy for Microsoft's anticompetitive conduct, as upheld by the Court of Appeals' decision.

The parties appeared before Judge Kollar-Kotelly for the first time at a conference held on September 28, 2001. The Court directed the parties to begin a settlement negotiation and mediation process, which would end on November 2. Specifically, the Court noted that " I expect [the parties] to engage in settlement discussions seven days a week around the clock in order to see if they can resolve this case." (Transcript of September 28, 2001 proceedings, page 5) The Court also adopted a detailed schedule governing the proceedings leading to a hearing on remedies, which the Court tentatively set for March 2002, if no settlement could be reached.

The settlement process that the District Court thus set in motion resulted in a proposed final judgment agreed to by Microsoft, DOJ and nine of the plaintiff States. The overarching objective of this settlement is to increase the choices available to consumers (including business users) who seek to buy PCs by promoting competition in the computer and computer software industries. More specifically (and as 1 will explain further below), the proposed final judgment includes the following means to increase consumer choice and industry competition:

- Microsoft will be prohibited from using various forms of conduct to punish or discourage industry participants from developing and offering products that compete or could compete with the Windows operating system, or with Microsoft software running on Windows.
- Microsoft will be prohibited from restricting the ability of computer manufacturers to make significant changes to Windows, thereby encouraging manufacturers to offer consumers more choice in the features included in PCs available for purchase.
- Microsoft will be required to disclose significant technical information that will help industry participants to develop and offer products that work well with Windows, and, in this way, potentially aid in the development of products that will compete with Windows itself.
- Microsoft will be subject to on-site scrutiny by a specially selected three person Committee, charged with responsibility to assist in enforcing Microsoft's obligations under the settlement, and to help resolve complaints and inquiries that arise by virtue of the settlement.

New York decided to settle the Microsoft case because we believe that the deal hammered out over the many weeks of negotiations will generate a more competitive marketplace for consumers and businesses throughout the country, and, indeed, throughout the world. In summary, the settlement that the parties have submitted to the District Court for approval will accomplish the following:

2. Empowering Computer Manufacturers to Offer Choices to Consumers

First, the proposed final judgment will empower computer manufacturers—the "OEMs"—to offer products that give consumers choice. Under the settlement, OEMs have the opportunity to add competing middleware to the Windows operating system in place of middleware included by Microsoft. (Section III, paragraphs C and H)[2] Middleware here refers not only to software like the Netscape browser, one of the subjects of the liability trial, but also to other important PC functions, such as email, instant messaging, or the media players that enable consumers to receive

[2] Parenthetical references are to Revised Proposed Final Judgment attached to the Stipulation, dated November 6, 2001 (the "November 6 Stipulation"), in *United States v. Microsoft Corp.*, Civil Action No. 98–1232 (CKK)(D.D.C.), and *State of New York v. Microsoft Corp.*, Civil Action No. 98–1233 (CKK)(D.D.C.) (together "Microsoft").

audio and visual content from the Internet. (Section VI, paragraphs K and M)[3] Middleware is important, in the context of this case, because it may help break down barriers that protect Microsoft's Windows monopoly.

The government negotiators insisted on, and eventually obtained, a broad definition of middleware so that the proposed decree covers both existing middleware and middleware not currently in existence, but which Microsoft and its competitors may develop during the term of the decree. The reason for our pressing a broad definition is plain enough: the broader the definition of middleware, the more software covered by the settlement, and the greater the opportunity for a software product to develop in a fashion that challenges the Windows monopoly.

Under the proposed decree, OEMs will have the ability to customize the PC's that they offer. They may, for example, add icons launching both competing middleware—and products that use competing middleware—to the Windows desktop or Start menu, and to other places in the Windows operating system. OEMs also will have the ability to suppress the existence of the competing middleware that Microsoft included in the Windows operating system licensed to the OEM. Microsoft itself will have to redesign Windows to the extent needed to permit this sort of substitution of middleware, and to ensure that the OEMs' customization of Windows is honored. (Section III, paragraphs C and H)[4]

The options available to OEMs under the settlement mean that the Windows desktop is up for sale. Companies offering a package of features that includes middleware, and middleware developers themselves, who desire to put their product into the hands of consumers can go to OEMs and buy a part of the real estate that the Windows desk top represents. This opportunity for additional revenue should further empower OEMs to develop competing computer products that offer choice to consumers.

The OEMs' ability to offer consumers competing middleware is backed up by a broad provision that prohibits Microsoft from "retaliating" against OEMs for any decision to install competing middleware (as well as any operating system that competes with Windows). (Section III, paragraph A) This provision forbids Microsoft from altering any of its commercial relations with an OEM, or from denying an OEM a wide array of product support or promotional benefits, based on the OEM's efforts to offer competitive alternatives. (Section VI, paragraph C)

Then, to back up the non-retaliation provision, Microsoft also is required to license Windows to its 20 largest OEMs (who comprise roughly 70% of new PC sales) under uniform, non-discriminatory terms. (Section III, paragraph B) Microsoft also is prohibited from terminating any of its 20 largest OEMs for Windows licensing violations without first giving the OEM notice and an opportunity to cure the alleged violation. (Section III, paragraph A)

3. Empowering Software Developers and Others to Offer Competing Middleware

Second, the proposed final judgment seeks to encourage independent software developers—referred to as "ISVs"—to write competing middleware. This is accomplished by forbidding Microsoft from retaliating against any IS V based on the ISV's efforts to introduce competing middleware or a competing operating system into the market. (Section III, paragraph F) The literally thousands of ISVs in the industry are protected by this additional non-retaliation provision, and they are protected whether or not they have an on-going business relationship with Microsoft.

ISVs, and many other industry participants, are further protected by provisions that prohibit Microsoft from entering into exclusive dealing arrangements relating to middleware or operating systems. Exclusive dealing arrangements are a device that Microsoft used to deny competitors access to the distribution lines needed to enable their products to gain acceptance in the marketplace. (Section III, paragraphs F, G) We have effectively closed off that practice to Microsoft.

4. Requiring Microsoft to Disclose Information to Facilitate Interoperation

Third, the proposed final judgment requires Microsoft to provide the technical information—"interfaces" and "protocols"—that industry members need to enable competing middleware to work well with Windows. Middleware uses functions of the Windows operating system through connections or "hooks" called "applications programming interfaces"—"APIs" for short. Microsoft will now be required to disclose

---

[3] For ease of exposition, I refer in this testimony to "middleware' as a generic term. In the proposed final judgment itself, there are four related middleware definitions, which are associated with various substantive provisions in the decree. (*See* Section VI, paragraphs J, K, M, N; Section IV(A) of the Competitive Impact Statement, dated November 15, 2001, filed in *Microsoft*.)

[4] PC users themselves will have a similar ability to customize Windows.

the APIs that its own middleware uses to interoperate with Windows, and to provide technical documents relating to those APIs, so that ISVs who wish to develop competing middleware will have the information needed to make their products work well with Windows. (Section III, paragraph D)

This is, again, a place where the broad definition of middleware, covering both existing and yet to be developed products, matters. (Section VI, paragraph J) The broader the definition, the greater the number of APIs that Microsoft must disclose and document. The greater the technical information made available, the greater the likelihood that industry participants will be able to develop competing middleware that works well on Windows.[5]

The proposed decree goes beyond requiring disclosure of APIs between Windows and Microsoft middleware. More and more, at-home consumers and computer users in the workplace can obtain functionality that they need from either the Internet or from network servers operating in a business setting. This trend means that computer applications running on servers may be an emerging location for developing middleware that could challenge the Windows monopoly at the PC level. Thus, the settlement is designed to prevent Microsoft from using Windows to gain competitive advantages in the way that PCs talk to servers. This is accomplished by requiring Microsoft to disclose, via a licensing mechanism, what are called "protocols" used to enable PCs and servers to communicate with each other. (Section III, paragraph E)

This particular provision—sometimes referred to as the "client/server interoperability" section—was especially important to the States. The provision included in the November 2 version of the final judgment between the DOJ and Microsoft did not seem to us in New York to go quite as far as we felt it needed to go. As a result, this was a place that we and other States focused on in the negotiations leading to the revised settlement signed on November 6. The changes that resulted did not involve many words, but we believe that they enhanced Microsoft's disclosure obligations in this critical area.

5. The Enforcement Mechanism

The subject matter of the Microsoft lawsuit is complex, and so too are many parts of the remedy embodied in the final judgment. This complexity creates the potential for good faith disagreement, as well as for intentional evasion. For this reason, from the outset of the settlement negotiations, New York held to the view that enforcement provisions going beyond those typically found in antitrust decrees would be needed here. We worked closely with DOJ to achieve this objective. What you find in the proposed final judgment is an enforcement mechanism that we believe is unprecedented in any antitrust case.

The proposed consent decree expressly recognizes the "exclusive responsibility" of the United States DOJ and the antitrust officials of the settling States to enforce the final judgment against Microsoft. (Section IV, paragraph A (1)) To assist this federal and state enforcement and compliance effort, the proposed decree will create a three person body, the "Technical Committee" or "TC." (Section IV, paragraph B) The TC is empowered, among other things: (1) to interview any Microsoft personnel; (2) to obtain copies of any Microsoft documents—including Microsoft's source code—and access to any Microsoft systems, equipment and physical facilities; and (3) to require Microsoft to provide compilations of documents, data and other information, and to prepare reports for the TC. (Section IV, paragraph B(8)(b), (c)) The TC itself is authorized to hire staff and consultants to carry out its responsibilities. (Section IV, paragraph B(8)(h)) Microsoft also is required to provide permanent office space and office support facilities for the TC at its Redmond, Washington campus. (Section IV, paragraph B(7))

In other words, for the five year term of the decree, the TC will be the on-site eyes and ears of the government enforcers. The TC and government enforcers may communicate with each other as often as they need to, and the TC may obtain advice or assistance from the enforcers on any matter within the TC's purview. In addition, the TC is subject to specific reporting requirements—every six months, or immediately if the TC finds any violation of the decree. (Section IV, paragraph B(8)(e),

[5] Strictly speaking, if Microsoft refrains from separately distributing a particular middleware product included in Windows, it need not disclose the APIs used by that middleware product. But powerful business considerations militate against Microsoft adopting a strategy in which *only* purchasers of new PCs, or of boxpackaged versions of Windows, receive a middleware product offered by Microsoft. Under such a strategy, Microsoft would be unable to supply the middleware product to *any* of the millions of Windows users worldwide who comprise its installed user base. Microsoft would thereby put itself at a competitive disadvantage as suppliers of competing middleware offered attractive product features to the installed base of Windows users.

(f)) The TC further will be expected to field and promptly resolve complaints and inquiries from industry members, or from government enforcers themselves. (Section IV, paragraph B(8)(d), paragraph D)

All of this will be paid for by Microsoft, subject to possible review by federal and state officials, or the Court. To discourage Microsoft from mounting dubious court challenges to the TC's costs and expenses, the proposed decree authorizes the TC to recover its litigation expenses, including attorneys' fees, unless the Court expressly finds that the TC's opposition was "without substantial justification." (Section IV, paragraph B(8)(i))

These enforcement provisions are probably the strongest ever crafted in an antitrust case. Federal and state enforcers will have at their disposal their regular enforcement powers, which may be invoked at any time independent of anything that the TC may do. (Section IV, paragraph A(2), (4)) Meanwhile, the TC will augment these traditional powers in significant respects. In addition, Microsoft itself is required to appoint an internal compliance officer to assist in assuring discharge of the company's obligations under the settlement. (Section IV, paragraph C)

I am mindful that concern has been expressed regarding the enforcement provision that "[n]o work product, findings or recommendations of the TC may be admitted in any enforcement proceeding before the Court . . . ." (Section IV, paragraph D(4)(d)) But the impact of this provision should not be great. As noted, the TC may report to the government enforcers, who may use the TC's work to seek from Microsoft a consensual resolution of, for example, any non-compliant conduct, to initiate (and inevitably shortcut) enforcement-looking activity, to pursue leads, and for other enforcement purposes. Moreover, the TC's work product, once known, should be readily susceptible of prompt replication by enforcement officials for use in judicial proceedings.

6. The Settlement Process

As the very fact of these hearings attests, the proposed settlement of the Microsoft case is a subject of significant public interest and debate. For years, many have asserted that the case itself should never have been filed to begin with. For these individuals, the government should be satisfied to get any remedy at all. We in New York profoundly disagree with this view. As the liability trial and appeal confirmed, this case was properly brought to remedy serious anticompetitive activity by Microsoft. The trial and appellate proceedings further confirmed that the antitrust laws are alive and well in technological industries, just as they are in other parts of our nation's economy. Accordingly, the public is entitled to a strong, effective remedy.

In this regard, however, some have criticized the settlement for not going far enough, or for having exceptions and limitations. We reject this view as well.

In announcing the decision by New York and eight other States to settle the case, New York Attorney General Eliot Spitzer noted that "a settlement is never perfect." A settlement is an agreed-upon resolution of competing positions and objectives. Do I wish that the DOJ and the States had gotten more? Of course I do. Do our counterparts on the Microsoft side wish that they had given up less? There is no doubt about the answer. So, asking these questions does not take us very far. Settlement necessarily means compromise. It is in the nature of the beast.

This particular settlement is the product of roughly five weeks of consuming negotiations, much of which took place under the guidance of two experienced mediators. I am unaware of any calculation of the total person-hours consumed by this effort. Certainly it was in the thousands, if not tens of thousands, of hours. The process required the two sides to explore, both internally and in face-to-face negotiations, a host of factors that bear on terms of the settlement eventually reached, such as: (1) the competitive consequences of varying courses of action; (2) the design, engineering and practical implications and limitations of various remedy approaches, as well as their impact on innovation incentives; (3) the issues actually framed for trial in the liability phase of the case and their resolution by the Court of Appeals; (4) the law governing remedies for the monopoly maintenance violation that the Court of Appeals upheld, which the District Court would be called on to apply in the absence of a settlement; and (5) the resources, effort and time otherwise needed to resolve the sharp factual disputes that would be presented in a full-blown remedies hearing. New York and the other States, as well as the DOJ, were aided in this process by experienced staff and retained experts.

In the final analysis, the DOJ, New York and the other settling States concluded that the benefits to consumers and to the competitive process that are likely to result from the negotiated settlement reached here outweigh the uncertain remedy that a contested remedies proceeding might bring. In assessing the soundness of that conclusion, the members of the Committee should recall that the settlement's critics have a luxury that those of us who settled did not have: they have the settlement floor created by the final judgment that we have offered. Absent this settlement, however, a judicial remedies hearing had not simply potential rewards, but significant risks as well.

During the September 28 court conference, the District Court expressed its views regarding the appropriate scope of the conduct remedies that might emerge from a judicial hearing on relief. Among other things, the District Court stated the following:

> The Supreme Court long ago stated that it's entirely appropriate for a district court to order a remedy which goes beyond a simple prescription against the precise conduct previously pursued . . . . The Supreme Court has vested this court with large discretion to fashion appropriate restraints both to avoid a recurrence of the violation and to eliminate its consequences. Now, case law in the antitrust field establishes that the exercise of discretion necessitates choosing from a range of alternatives.
>
> * * *
>
> So the government's first and most obvious task is going to be to determine which portions of the former judgment remain appropriate in light of the appellate court's ruling and which portions are unsupported following the appellate court's narrowing of liability.
>
> Now, the scope of any proposed remedy must be carefully crafted so as to ensure that the enjoining conduct falls within the number [*sic*, penumbra] of behavior which was found to be anticompetitive. The government will also have to be cautiously attentive to the efficacy of every element of the proposed relief.

(Transcript of September 28, 2001 proceedings, pages 9, 8)

These remarks highlight risks that both sides confronted if the decision were made to press for a court-ordered remedy. Several concrete examples, from the settlement actually reached, will further drive home this point.

- Microsoft's API disclosure obligations, and its obligations to permit OEMs to customize the Windows desktop and operating system more generally, revolve around a series of related middleware definitions that the parties agreed to. Absent a settlement, there could no assurance that the courts would adopt middleware definitions as broad as those that DOJ and the settling States negotiated.
- The liability trial in the case centered on Microsoft's conduct directed to efforts by Netscape and Sun to get Netscape's web browser and Sun's Java technologies installed on individual PCs. Plaintiffs' theory of the case—which the trial and appellate courts upheld—was that these forms of middleware could, if sufficiently pervasive at the PC level, erode the applications barrier to entry that protects Microsoft's Windows monopoly. Microsoft therefore set out to exclude this middleware from PCs. In the settlement negotiations leading to the client/server interoperability provision, the government negotiators argued that applications running at the server level can be analogous to middleware running at the PC level. On this approach, middleware developed at the server level could also break down the applications barrier to entry into the PC operating system market. Therefore, the remedy in this case requires Microsoft to disclose ways that PCs running Windows talk to servers running Microsoft software. Absent a settlement, however, there could be no assurance that the courts would order disclosure of this PC/server line of communications. Microsoft resisted this provision during the settlement negotiations, and would similarly have opposed it at a remedies hearing.
- Finally, as I noted above, there does not seem to be any antitrust precedent for an enforcement mechanism that puts a monitor on site, with full access to the defendant's documents, employees, systems and physical facilities—all at the defendant's expense. Absent a settlement, Microsoft would have vigorously opposed such a far-reaching enforcement regime, and there plainly could be no assurance that the courts would have ordered comparable relief.

As these examples reflect, I believe that the proposed final judgment compares favorably to—and in some respects may well exceed—the remedy that might have emerged from a judicial hearing.

The existence of a settlement has also accelerated the point in time at which a remedy will begin to take effect. Microsoft has agreed to begin complying with the proposed final judgment starting on December 16, 2001. (November 6 Stipulation, paragraph 2) Assuming further that the District Court approves the proposed final judgment in Tunney Act proceedings in early 2002, there will be a remedy in place a year or more before the trial and appellate level proceedings, needed to resolve the appropriate remedy in the absence of a settlement, would be concluded. In this rapidly changing sector of the industry, the timeliness of a remedy is an important consideration.

7. Conclusion

In sum, the settlement in the Microsoft case promotes competition and consumer choice. It is proportionate to the monopoly maintenance violations that the Court of Appeals for the District of Columbia Circuit sustained. The settlement represents a fair and reasonable vindication of the public interest in assuring the free and open competition that our nation's antitrust laws guarantee.

Microsoft is reported recently to have issued a company-wide email stating its commitment to making the settlement "a success" and to "ensuring that everyone at Microsoft complies fully with the terms" of the decree. D.]an Hopper, Associated Press State & Local Wire (Nov. 30, 2001). We expect nothing less, and we intend to see to it that Microsoft honors that commitment. New York is one of the members of the States' enforcement Committee, created under the proposed decree. Our State Antitrust Bureau will be vigilant in monitoring Microsoft's discharge of its obligations, and we look forward to working closely with the DOJ to make sure that the settlement is, indeed, a success. The American public is entitled to nothing less.

Statement of Hon. Jon Kyl, a U.S. Senator from the State of Arizona

Mr. Chairman:

The five-year judicial proceeding in the *United States v. Microsoft* litigation may be approaching a conclusion. Final briefs have been submitted and final arguments have been heard by Judge Colleen Kollar-Kotelly of the U.S. District Court of the District of Columbia on the issue of whether to affirm, reject, or modify the settlement reached between Microsoft, the Department of Justice, and nine settling states.

It is unclear when a decision will be handed down, or whether the decision, whatever it may be, will be appealed by any or all of the parties. However, it is important to note that Judge Kotelly, a Clinton appointee, has from the bench expressed strong support for a settlement.

I offer my view as a U.S. Senator and as a member of the legislative branch of our government, a government in which the constitutional separation of legislative, judicial, and executive powers is scrupulously maintained. My purpose is not to influence the ongoing judicial process; rather, it is to offer my views to the Committee in a hearing which could be viewed as one-sided in opposition to the settlement.

My view is that the parties have reached a balanced remedy for Microsoft's anticompetitive conduct. I believe this settlement is in the public interest because it will promote vigorous competition to the benefit of all consumers, and will advance the public policy codified in the Sherman Anti-Trust Act, which is to protect competition—not competitors.

This settlement will, by its terms, effectively force Microsoft to reform how it conducts its business through comprehensive oversight and enforcement provisions. Those terms seem appropriate to the court's findings.

Specifically, I am persuaded by the testimony of Assistant Attorney General for Antitrust, Charles James, that this is a timely settlement which remedies Microsoft's antitrust violations within the scope of the appellate court's ruling that Microsoft illegally maintained its Windows operating system monopoly. "We wanted to stop the violations now, not after years of further proceedings and appeals," said Mr. James.

The settlement forces several key concessions upon Microsoft for violating Section 2 of the Sherman Act. For instance, under its terms, the settlement affords makers of personal computers wide latitude to install non-Microsoft software on new computers, and to remove access to Microsoft icons and features, such as Internet browsers. It also forbids retaliation against companies that utilize this new latitude.

The settlement also prohibits exclusive contracts, and requires that Microsoft disclose proprietary hardware and software design-code information so that competing products can be manufactured that are completely compatible with the Windows operating system. Significantly, the five-year settlement also establishes an independent technical compliance Committee that will assume permanent residency on the Microsoft campus to monitor compliance with the terms of this settlement.

This compliance Committee will have full access to the facilities, personnel, records, and intellectual property of Microsoft. And, it is important to note that oversight of the independent compliance Committee is complementary to, not in place of, the ongoing oversight of the Department of Justice and the settling states.

Mr. Chairman, in sum, I believe this settlement will protect and cultivate a vigorous and competitive computer soft and hardware industry. Such competition is integral to the health and vitality of the U.S. economy, and is in the clear interests of the American consumer.

I will readily accept the final judicial resolution of this case, whatever it may be. Thank you, Mr. Chairman.

Statement of Professor Lawrence Lessig, Esq., Stanford Law School, Stanford, California

Four years after the United States government initiated legal action against the Microsoft Corporation, Microsoft, the federal government, and nine states have agreed upon a consent decree ("the proposed decree") to settle the finding of antitrust liability that the Court of Appeals for the D.C. Circuit has unanimously affirmed. In my view, that consent decree suffers from a significant, if narrow, flaw. While it properly enlists the market as the ultimate check on Microsoft's wrongful behavior, it fails to provide an adequate mechanism of enforcement to implement its requirements. If it is adopted without modification, it will fail to achieve the objectives that the government had when it brought this case.

Yet while it is important that an adequate and effective remedy be imposed against Microsoft, in my view it equally important that any remedy not be extreme. Microsoft is no longer the most significant threat to innovation on the Internet. Indeed, as I explain more fully below, under at least one understanding of its current Internet strategy, Microsoft could well play a crucial role in assuring a strong and neutral platform for innovation in the future. Thus, rather than retribution, a remedy should aim to steer the company toward this benign and beneficial strategy. Obviously, this benign understanding of Microsoft's current strategy is not the only understanding. Nor do I believe that anyone should simply trust Microsoft to adopt it. But its possibility does suggest the importance of balance in any remedy. The proposed decree does not achieve that balance, but neither, in my view, does the alternative.

I am a law professor at Stanford Law School and have written extensively about the interaction between law and technology. My most recent book addresses directly the effect of law and technology on innovation. I have also been involved in the proceedings of this case. In 1997, I was appointed special master in the action to enforce the 1995 consent decree. That appointment was vacated by the Court of Appeals when it concluded that the powers granted me exceeded the scope of the special master statute. *United States v. Microsoft Corporation*, 147 F.3d 935, 953–56 (D.C. Cir 1998) ("Microsoft II"). I was then invited by the District Court to submit a brief on the question of using software code to "tie" two products together.[1] I have subsequently spent a great deal of time studying the case and its resolution.

In this testimony, I outline the background against which I draw my conclusions. I then consider the proposed decree, and some of the strengths and weaknesses of the alternative proposed to the District Court by the nine remaining states (the "alternative"). Finally, I consider two particular areas in which this Committee may usefully consider action in light of the experience in this case.

BACKGROUND

In June, 2001, the Court of Appeals for the D.C. Circuit unanimously affirmed Judge Jackson's conclusion that Microsoft used its power over Windows to protect itself against innovation that threatened its monopoly power. *United States v. Microsoft Corporation*, 253 F.3d 54 (D.C. Cir 2001) (Microsoft III). That behavior, the Court concluded, violated the nation's antitrust laws. The Court therefore ordered the District Court to craft a remedy that would "'unfetter [the] market from anticompetitive conduct,' to 'terminate the illegal monopoly, deny to the defendant the fruits of its statutory violation, and ensure that there remain no practices likely to result in monopolization in the future.'" *Microsoft III*, 253 F.2d at 103 (citations omitted).

Integral to the Court's conclusion was its finding that Microsoft had "commingled code" in such a way as to interfere with the ability of competitors to offer equivalent

[1] See <http://cyberlaw.stanford.edu/lessig/content/testimony/ab/ab.pdf>.

products on an even playing field. As the District Court found, and the Court of Appeals affirmed, Microsoft had designed its products in such a way as to inhibit the substitution of certain product functionality. This design, the district court concluded, served no legitimate business interest. The Court's conclusion was therefore that Microsoft had acted strategically to protect its market power against certain forms of competition.

In my view, this holding by the Court of Appeals is both correct and important. It vindicates a crucial principle for the future of innovation generally, and in particular, on the Internet. By affirming the principle that no company with market power may use its power over a platform to protect itself against competition, the Court has assured competitors in this and other fields that the ultimate test of success for their products is not the decision by a platform owner, but the choice of consumers using the product. To the extent that Microsoft's behavior violated this principle, and continues to violate this principle, it is appropriate for the District Court to craft a remedy that will stop that violation.

An appropriate remedy, however, must take into account the competitive context at the time the remedy is imposed. And in my view, it is crucially important to see that Microsoft does not represent the only, or even the most significant, threat to innovation on the Internet. If the exercise of power over a platform to protect that platform owner from competition is a threat to innovation (as I believe the Court of Appeals has found), then there are other actors who also have significant power over aspects of the Internet platform who could also pose a similarly dangerous threat to the neutral platform for innovation that the Internet as has been. For example, broadband cable could become a similar threat to innovation, if access to the Internet through cable is architected so as to give cable the power to discriminate among applications and content. Similarly, as Chairman Michael Powell suggested in a recent speech about broadband technology, overly protective intellectual property laws could well present a threat to broadband deployment.[2]

Microsoft could play a significant role in resisting this kind of corruption of the Internet's basic values, and could therefore play an important role in preserving the environment for innovation on the net. In particular, under one understanding of Microsoft's current Internet strategy (which I will refer to generally as the ".NET strategy"), Microsoft's architecture would push computing power and network control to the "edge" or "ends" of the network, and away from the network's core. This is consistent with a founding design principle of the early network—what network architects Jerome Saltzer, David Clark, and David Reed call "the end-to-end argument."[3] .NET'S possible support of this principle would compete with pressures that now encourage a compromise of the end-to-end design. To the extent Microsoft's strategy resists that compromise, it could become a crucial force in preserving the innovation of the early network.

This is not to say that this benign, pro-competitive design is the only way that Microsoft could implement its .NET strategy. There are other implementations that could certainly continue Microsoft's present threat to competition. And obviously, I am not arguing that anyone should trust Microsoft's representation that it intends one kind of implementation over another. Trust alone is not an adequate remedy to the current antitrust trial.

My point instead is that there is little reason to vilify a company with a strong and powerful interest in a strategy that might well reinforce competition on the Internet—especially when, excepting the open source and free software companies presently competing with Microsoft, few of the other major actors have revealed a similarly proInternet strategy. Thus, rather than adopting a remedy that is focused exclusively on the "last war," a proper remedy to the current antitrust case should be sufficient to steer Microsoft towards its benign strategy, while assuring an adequate response if it fails to follow this procompetitive lead.

Such a remedy must be strong but also effectively and efficiently enforceable. The fatal weakness in the proposed decree is not so much the extent of the restrictions on Microsoft's behavior, as it is the weaknesses in the proposed mechanisms for enforcement. Fixing that flaw is no doubt necessary to assure an adequate decree. In my view, it may also be sufficient.

---

[2] See <http://www.fcc.gov/Speeches/Powell/2001/spmkp110.html> (suggesting "re-examining the copyright laws" and comparing freedom assured by decision permitting VCRs).

[3] See *End to End Arguments in System Design*, <http://web.mit.edu/Saltzer/www/publications/>.

THE PROPOSED DECREE

While the proposed decree is not a model of clarity, the essence of its strategy is simply stated: To use the market to police Microsoft's monopoly. The decree does this by assuring that computer manufacturers and software vendors remain free to bundle and support non-Microsoft software without fear of punishment by Microsoft. Dell or Compaq are thus guaranteed the right to bundle browsers from Netscape or media players from Apple regardless of the mix that Microsoft has built into Windows. Autonomy from Microsoft is thus the essence of the plan—the freedom to include any "middleware" software with an operating system regardless of whether or not it benefits Microsoft.

If this plan could be made to work, it would be the ideal remedy to this four year struggle. Government regulators can't know what should or should not be in an operating system. The market should make that choice. And if competitors and computer manufacturers could be assured that they can respond to the demands of the market without fear of retaliation by Microsoft, then in my view they would play a sufficient role in checking any misbehavior by Microsoft.

The weakness in the proposed decree, however, is its failure to specify any effective mechanism for assuring that Microsoft complies. The central lesson that regulators should have learned from this case is the inability of the judicial system to respond quickly enough to violations of the law.

Thus the first problem that any proposed decree should have resolved is a more efficient way to assure that Microsoft complies with the decree's requirements. Under the existing system for enforcement, by the time a wrong is adjudicated, the harm of the wrong is complete.

Yet the proposed decree does nothing to address this central problem. The decree does not include provision for a special master, or panel of masters, to assure that disagreements about application could be quickly resolved. Nor does it provide an alternative fast-track enforcement mechanism to guarantee compliance.

Instead the decree envisions the creation of a Committee of technical experts, trained in computer programming, who will oversee Microsoft's compliance. But while such expertise is necessary in the ongoing enforcement of the decree, equally important will be the interpretation and application of the decree to facts as they arise. This role cannot be played by technical experts, and yet in my view,this is the most important role in the ongoing enforcement of the decree.

For example, the decree requires that Microsoft not retaliate against an independent software vendor because that vendor develops or supports products that compete with Microsoft's. Proposed Decree, § III.B. By implication, this means Microsoft would be free to retaliate for other reasons unrelated to the vendor's competing software. Whether a particular act was "retaliation" for an improper purpose is not a technical question. It is an interpretive question calling upon the skills of a lawyer. To resolve that question would therefore require a different set of skills from those held by members of the technical Committee.

The remedy for this weakness is a better enforcement mechanism. As the nine remaining states have suggested, a special master with the authority to interpret and apply the decree would assure a rapid and effective check on Microsoft's improper behavior. While I suggest some potential problems with the appointment of a special master in the final section of this testimony, this arrangement would assure effective monitoring of Microsoft, subject to appeal to the District Court.

The failure to include an effective enforcement mechanism is, in my view, the fatal weakness in the proposed decree. And while I agree with the nine remaining states that there are other weaknesses as well, in my view these other weaknesses are less important than this single flaw. More specifically, in my view, were the decree modified to assure an effective enforcement mechanism, then it may well suffice to assure the decree's success. Without this modification, there is little more than faith to assure that this decree will work. With this modification, even an incompletely specified decree may suffice.

The reason, in my view, is that even a partial, yet effectively enforced decree, could be sufficient to steer Microsoft away from strategic behavior harmful to competition. Even if every loophole is not closed, if the decree can be effectively enforced, then it could suffice to push Microsoft towards a benign, pro-competitive strategy. The proposed decree has certainly targeted the most important opportunity for strategic, or anti-competitive, behavior. If the chance to act on these without consequence is removed, then in my view, Microsoft has a strong incentive to focus its future behavior towards an implementation of its .NET strategy that would reinforce rather than weaken the competitive field. An effective, if incomplete, decree could, in other words, suffice to drive Microsoft away from the pattern of strategic behavior that has been proven against it in the Court of Appeals.

There are those who believe Microsoft will adopt this benign strategy whether or not there is a remedy imposed against them. Indeed, some within Microsoft apparently believe that supporting a neutral open platform is in the best interests of the company.[4] Given the significant findings of liability affirmed by the Court of Appeals, I do not believe it is appropriate to leave these matters to faith. But I do believe that a remedy can tilt Microsoft towards this better strategy, at least if the remedy can be efficiently enforced.

THE NINE STATES' ALTERNATIVE

On Friday, December 7, 2001, the nine states that have not agreed to the proposed consent decree outlined an alternative remedy to the one proposed by the Justice Department. In many ways, I believe this alternative is superior to the Justice Department's proposed decree. This alternative more effectively protects against a core strategy attacked in the District Court—the commingling of code designed to protect Microsoft's monopoly power. It has an effective enforcement provision, envisioning the appointment of a special master. The alternative has a much stronger mechanism for adding competition to the market—by requiring that Microsoft continue to market older versions of its operating system in competition with new versions. And finally, the alternative requires that Microsoft continue to distribute Java technologies as its has in prior Windows versions.

The alternative, however, goes beyond what in my view is necessary. And while in light of the past, erring on the side of overly protective remedies might make sense, I will describe a few areas where the alternative may have gone too far, after a brief description of a few of the differences that I believe are genuine improvements.

Areas of Common Strategy

Both the proposed decree and the alternative agree on a common set of strategies for restoring competition in the market place. Both seek to assure autonomy for computer manufacturers and software vendors to bundle products on the Microsoft platform differently according to consumer demand. Both decrees aim at that end by guaranteeing nondiscriminatory licensing practices, and restrictions on retaliation against providers who bundle or support non-Microsoft products. The alternative specifies this strategy more cleanly than the proposed decree. It is also more comprehensive. But both are aiming rightly at the same common end: to empower competitors to check Microsoft's power.

Improvements of the Alternative

The alternative remedy adds features to the proposed decree that are in my view beneficial. Central among these is the more effective enforcement mechanism. The alternative proposes the establishment of a special master, with sufficient authority to oversee compliance. This, as I've indicated, is a necessary condition of any successful decree, and may also be sufficient.

Beyond this significant change, however, there are a number of valuable additions in the states' alternative. By targeting the "binding" of middleware to the operating system, the alternative more effectively addresses a primary concern of the Court of Appeals. This restriction assures that Microsoft does not architect its software in a way that enables it strategically to protect itself against competition. Such binding was found by the courts to make it costly for users to select competing functionality, without any compensating pro-competitive benefit.

The alternative also assures much greater competition with new versions of the Windows operating system by requiring that prior versions continue to be licensed by Microsoft. This competition would make it harder for Microsoft to use its monopoly power to push users to adopt new versions of the operating system that advance Microsoft's strategic objectives, but not consumer preferences.

Finally, the alternative addresses a troubling decision by Microsoft to refuse to distribute Java technologies with Windows XP. This decision by Microsoft raises a significant concern that Microsoft is determined to continue to play strategically to strengthen the applications barrier to entry.

Concerns about the proposed alternative

While I believe the alternative represents a significant improvement over the proposed consent decree, I am concerned that the alternative may go beyond the proper scope of the remedy.

---

[4] This is the argument of David Bank's *Breaking Windows: How Bill Gates Fumbled the Future of Microsoft* (New York: Free Press, 2001).

Open Sourcing Internet Explorer: While I am a strong supporter of the free and open source software movements, and believe software of both varieties is unlikely ever to pose any of the same strategic threats that closed source software does, I am not convinced the requirement of open sourcing Internet Explorer is yet required, or even effective. Both proposed remedies have a strong requirement that application interfaces be disclosed, and until that remedy proves incomplete, I don't believe the much more extreme requirement of full disclosure of source code is merited.

The definition of Middleware Products: The central target of the litigation was Microsoft's behavior with respect to middleware software. Understood in terms relevant to this case, middleware software is software that lowers the applications barrier to entry *by reducing the cost of cross-compatibility*. Java tied to the Netscape browser is an example of middleware so understood; had it been successfully and adequately deployed, it would have made it easier for application program developers to develop applications that were operating system agnostic, and therefore would have increased the demand for other competing operating systems.

This definition is consistent with the alternative definition of "middleware." But the specification of "middleware products" reaches, in my view, beyond the target of "middleware." Middleware is not properly understood as software that increases the number of cross-platform applications; middleware is software that increases the ease with which cross-platform programs can be written. Thus, for example, Office is not middleware simply because it is a cross-platform program. It would only qualify as middleware if it made it easier for programmers to write platform-agnostic code.

The requirement that Office be ported: For a similar reason, I am not convinced of the propriety of requiring that Office be ported. While Office for the Macintosh is certainly a crucial application for the continued viability of the Macintosh OS, having Office on many platforms does not significantly affect the applications barrier to entry. No doubt if Microsoft strategically pulled the development of Office in order to defeat another operating system, or if it aggressively resisted applications that were designed to be compatible with Office (such as Sun's Star Office), that could raise antitrust concerns. But the failure simply to develop office for another platform would not itself respond to the concerns of the Court of Appeals.

No doubt, each of these additional remedies might be conceived of as necessary prophylactics given a judgment that Microsoft is resolved to continue its strategic anticompetitive behavior. And after a fair and adequate hearing in the District Court, such a prophylactic may well prove justified. At this stage, however, I am not convinced these have been proven necessary.

APPROPRIATE CONGRESSIONAL ACTION

It is obviously inappropriate for Congress to intervene in an ongoing legal dispute with the intent to alter the ultimate judgment of the judicial process. Thus while I believe it is extremely helpful and important that this Committee review the matters at stake at this time, there is a limit to what this Committee can properly do. In a system of separated powers, Congress does not sit in judgment over decisions by Courts.

Yet there are two aspects to this case that do justify a greater concern by Congress. Both aspects are intimately tied to earlier decisions by the Court of Appeals. First, in light of the Court of Appeals' judgment in the 1995 Microsoft litigation, *United States v. Microsoft Corporation*, 56 F.3d 1448 (D.C. Cir. 1995) (Microsoft I), it is clear that the Tunney Act proceedings before the District Court are extraordinarily narrow. Second, in light of the Court of Appeals' judgment in 1998 Microsoft litigation, *Microsoft II*, it is not clear that, absent consent of the parties, the District Court has the power to appoint a special master with the necessary authority to assure enforcement of any proposed remedy. Both concerns may justify this Committee taking an especially active role to assure a proper judgment can be reached—in the first case through its consultation with the executive, and the second, possibly with clearer legislative authority.

The Tunney Act Proceedings

In *Microsoft I*, the Court of Appeals for the D. C. Circuit held that the District Court's authority under the Tunney Act to question a consent decree proposed by the government was exceptionally narrow. Though that statute requires that the District Court assure that any consent decree is "within the public interest," the Court read that standard to be extremely narrow. If the decree can be said to be within "the reaches of the public interest," *Microsoft I*, 56 F.3d at 1461, then it is to be upheld.

The consequence of this holding is that it will be especially hard for the District Court to question the government's proposed decree. Absent a showing of corruption, the decree must be affirmed. It is hard for me to imagine that the proposed decree would fail this extremely deferential standard. Thus any weaknesses in the proposed decree would have to be resolved in the parallel proceedings being pursued by the nine states.

This deference may be a reason for Congress in the future to revisit the standard under the Tunney Act. Such a review could not properly affect this case, but concerns about this case may well suggest the value in future contexts.

But the concern about this decree may well be relevant to this Committee's view about the appropriateness of the government's cooperation with any ongoing prosecution by the nine states. The federal government may well have decided its remedy is enough; it wouldn't follow from that determination that the federal government has a reason to oppose the stronger remedies sought by the states. At a minimum, the government should free advisors or consultants it has worked with to aid the continuing states as they may desire.

The power to appoint a "special master"

In Microsoft II, the Court of Appeals interpreted a District Court's power to appoint a special master quite narrowly. While the Court acknowledged the strong tradition of using special masters to enforce judgments, it raised doubt about the power of the special master to act beyond essentially ministerial tasks. In particular, the task of interpreting and applying a consent decree to contested facts was held by the Court of Appeals to be beyond the statute's power—at least where the District Court did not reserve to itself de novo review of the special master's determination. *Microsoft II*, 147 F.3d at 953–56.

This narrow view of a special master's power was a surprise to many. It may well interfere with the ability of District Courts to utilize masters in highly technical or complex cases. This Committee may well need to consider whether more expansive authority should be granted the District Courts. Especially in the context of highly technical cases, a properly appointed master can provide invaluable assistance to the District Court judge.

These limitations would not, of course, restrict the appointment of a master in any case to which the parties agreed. And it may well be that the simplest way for Microsoft to achieve credibility in the context of this case would be for it to agree to the appointment of a master with substantial authority to interpret and apply the decree, subject to de novo review by the District Court. Such a master should be well trained in the law, but also possess a significant degree of technical knowledge. But beyond the particulars of this case, it may well be better if the District Court had greater power to call upon such assistance if such the Court deemed such assistance necessary.

Statement of Mitchell E. Kertzman, Chief Executive Officer, Liberate Technologies, San Carlos, California

Introduction

Mr. Chairman, Senator Hatch, and other members of the Committee, thank you for the chance to speak on this critical topic. The Proposed Final Judgment is woefully inadequate. It is a backward-looking document that fails to prevent Microsoft from abusing its monopoly position to increase costs and stifle new technologies—not just for personal computers, but also for new technologies like digital televisions, cellular phones, game consoles, and personal digital assistants.

Microsoft has already announced its intent to expand its dominance beyond PC operating systems, servers, and applications to new devices and even personal information via its "eHome" and "Passport" initiatives. According to comments made by Microsoft President Steve Ballmer just last week, Microsoft is pursuing a 'broader concept" for its client devices like the xBox and set-top box software. In his words, "[T]here's a bigger play we hope to get over time" by annexing all of these devices into the Microsoft empire. Microsoft's own demos and white papers show that it plans to establish its operating system as the software that would collect information streaming into the home and distribute it to each new device.

Microsoft has used and will continue to use its monopoly over desktop operating systems to deny competition in each new computing market as it evolves: first desktop applications, then internet browsers and servers, and now alternative devices ranging from smart phones to television set-top boxes.

By dealing only with a narrow category of Windows products, and failing even there to impose any significant restrictions, the Proposed Final Judgment fails to check Microsoft's demonstrated willingness to exploit its power over the operating system in order to dominate other market segments.

Background

By way of personal background, I am the CEO of Liberate Technologies, a company making middleware software that enables interactive and enhanced television. Before joining Liberate, I was Chairman and CEO of Sybase, then one of the world's ten largest independent software companies, founder and CEO of Powersoft, an enterprise software company, and Chairman of both the American Electronics Association and the Massachusetts Software Council. I am also currently a director of CNET, Handspring, and TechNet.

Throughout my career, I have both partnered with and competed against Microsoft. I have been impressed by the power of its dominant platforms, but also concerned about the abuses that resulted from that dominance. I have seen Microsoft consistently use its power to block competition in new markets through at least three types of misconduct that the PFJ does nothing to deter: (1) Preventing original equipment manufacturers from supporting new technologies; (2) Tying commercial restrictions to investments; and (3) Blocking non-Windows-based industry standards.

(1) Preventing Original Equipment Manufacturers from Supporting New Technologies

My current company, Liberate, was originally Network Computer Incorporated, promoting computers and software that would operate via a network to significantly reduce the cost of computing. This model, like the Netscape browser, threatened the dominance of the Windows platform. But because the manufacturers of many new devices also manufacture desktop PCs, Microsoft was able to exploit its desktop OEM relationships to discourage competition. For example, Network Computer had an active relationship with Digital Equipment Corporation to develop a device running our software. Microsoft and Mr. Gates simply threatened the CEO of DEC that they would port Microsoft's NT operating system to DEC hardware only if DEC stopped development of a network computer, an offer DEC couldn't refuse. It's clear, and the courts have reaffirmed, that a monopoly simply cannot engage in this kind of conduct.

Such tactics forced us to exit this business, and the price of PC operating systems and applications remains as high as ever when all other computing costs have plummeted.

The Proposed Final Judgment focuses only on Windows products for desktop PCs and includes broad and ambiguous exceptions to its limits on retaliation. These loopholes would apparently let Microsoft get away with the kind of misconduct it perpetrated against Network Computer. The result would be to block or delay the development of new competitive devices and technologies. The remedy proposed by the non-settling states would, on the other hand, prevent Microsoft from engaging in this type of retaliation and unfairly extending its desktop monopoly to a wider array of software and devices.

Tying Commercial Restrictions to Investments

Second, in investing the considerable proceeds of its desktop monopoly in new markets, Microsoft has extracted, or attempted to extract, exclusive or near-exclusive commercial distribution arrangements to block out competitors. In the interactive television industry alone, Microsoft has invested billions of dollars with leading cable and satellite networks. As recently as this week, Microsoft has again aggressively pursued this strategy with leading operators both here and in Europe. The strings attached to these investments often require networks to buy Microsoft's middleware, making it difficult or impossible for them to buy competitive products.

Microsoft's money is a heavy thumb on the scale, biasing choices of future technologies in its favor. As new-generation computers and small consumer devices often rely on networks for their interconnections, these investments in network companies set the stage for continued dominance of these new platforms as they evolve.

Again, the PFJ fails to even address the issue of such restrictive dealings outside the scope of desktop products. In contrast, the remedies filed last week by the non-settling states, while not barring new investments, would at least require that Microsoft give 60 days notice to permit a review of anti-competitive effects.

(3) Refusing to Support Non-Windows-Based Industry Standards

Microsoft has also abused its monopoly position by blocking industry-wide standards essential to the evolution of a new generation of network-based devices. In our industry, Microsoft has undermined Java as a standard for digital television, lobbying heavily to prevent U.S. and European standards bodies from standardizing on Java. As you know, Java lets developers "write once, run anywhere", permitting content to run across a wide variety of platforms rather than just on Microsoft's proprietary code.

As a second prong of this strategy to block, co-opt, or "embrace and extend" standards, Microsoft has refused to join with other technology companies in pooling its intellectual property, instead indicating that it will sue to block the implementation of standards wherever it can find a violation of one of its patents. Microsoft certainly has the right not to support a standard. However, they are exploiting their dominance in the PC market to distort standards elsewhere.

Third, by removing the Java Virtual machine from its PC operating systems while the JVM is common elsewhere, Microsoft discourages developers from creating new "write-once, run-anywhere" content, undermines support for uniform standards, and drives developers to write to proprietary Microsoft platforms.

It is clear that Microsoft's foot-dragging and affirmative interference has slowed the deployment of digital television in the United States. Cable companies and television manufacturers both say that a gating issue has been the lack of a definitive standard for digital television, a standard that Microsoft's tactics have delayed and undermined. Microsoft's approach stands in direct opposition to the clearly expressed will of Congress and the interests of all Americans interested in richer and more varied television programming.

Yet again, the PFJ would do nothing to prevent these abuses. The remedies recently filed by the non-settling states—by making available Microsoft APIs and certain types of code, opening access to the personal identification data captured by Microsoft Passport, and requiring the distribution of the Java Virtual Machine—would promote technology interoperability and the development of universally beneficial standards while maintaining relatively open alternatives to Microsoft software and services.

Conclusion

The PFJ is a disappointment. Disappointing because it is weaker than the facts and the law of the case support, and disappointing because it will not limit Microsoft's plans to dominate new markets in the same way it has dominated operating systems, applications, and servers in the past.

I welcome this hearing, and hope that this Committee will continue to exercise vigorous oversight of this case to assure that the final outcome is in the best interests of American consumers.

Statement of Charles F. (Rick) Rule, Counsel, Fried, Frank, Harris, Shriver & Jacobson, Counsel for Microsoft Corporation, Washington, D.C.

Mr. Chairman and members of the Committee, good morning. It is a pleasure to appear before you today on behalf of Microsoft Corporation to discuss the proposed consent decree or Revised Proposed Final Judgment (the "PFJ") to which the U.S. Department of Justice and nine of the plaintiff states have agreed. As this Committee is aware, I am counsel to Microsoft in the case and was one of the principal representatives for the company in the negotiations that led to the proposed consent decree.

The PFJ was signed on November 6th after more than a month of intense, around the clock negotiations with the Department and representatives of all the plaintiff states. The decree is currently subject to a public interest review by Judge Kollar-Kotelly under the Tunney Act[1]. Because we are currently in the midst of that review and because nine states and the District of Columbia have chosen to continue the litigation, I must be somewhat circumspect in my remarks. However, what I can—indeed, must—stress is that, in light of the Court of Appeals' decision last summer to "drastically" reduce the scope of Microsoft's liability and in light of the legal standards for imposing injunctive relief, the Department and the settling states were very effective in negotiating for broad, strong relief. As the chart in the appendix depicts, ever since the Department and the plaintiff states first filed their complaints in May 1998, the case has been shrinking. What began with five claims, was whittled down to a single monopoly maintenance claim by a unanimous Court of Appeals. Even with respect to that surviving claim, the appellate court affirmed

[1] 15 U.S.C. § 16(b)–(h).

Judge Jackson's findings on only about a third (12 of 35) of the specific acts which the district court had found support that claim.

Given that history and the law, there is no reasonable argument that the PFJ is too narrow or that it fails to achieve all the relief to which the Department was entitled. In fact, as these remarks explain, the opposite is true—faced with tough, determined negotiators on the other side of the table, Microsoft agreed to a decree that goes substantially beyond what the plaintiffs were likely to achieve through litigation. Quite frankly, the PFJ is the strongest, most regulatory conduct decree ever obtained (through litigation or settlement) by the Department.

Why then, one might ask, would Microsoft consent to such a decree? There are two reasons. First, the company felt strongly that it was important to put this matter behind it and to move forward constructively with its customers, its business partners, and the government. For four years, the litigation has consumed enormous resources and been a serious distraction. The constant media drumbeat has obscured the fact that the company puts a premium on adhering to its legal obligations and on developing and maintaining excellent relationships with its partners and customers. Litigation is never a pleasant experience, and given the magnitude of this case and the media attention it attracted, it is hard to imagine any more costly, unpleasant civil litigation.

Second, while the Department pushed Microsoft to make substantial, even excessive concessions to get a settlement, there were limits to how far the company was willing or able to go (limits, by the way, which the Department and the settling states managed to reach). Microsoft was fighting for an important principle—the ability to innovate and improve its products and services for the benefit of consumers. To that end, Microsoft insisted that the decree be written in a way to allow the company to engage in legitimate competition on the merits. Despite the substantial burdens the decree will impose on Microsoft and the numerous ways in which Microsoft will be forced to alter its conduct, the decree does preserve Microsoft's ability to innovate, to improve its products, and to engage in procompetitive business conduct that is necessary for the company to survive.

In short, at the end of the negotiations, Microsoft concluded that the very real costs that the decree imposes on the company are outweighed by the benefits, not just to Microsoft but to the PC industry and consumers generally.

The Court of Appeals' "Road Map" for Relief

In order to evaluate the decree, one must first appreciate the history of this case and how drastically the scope of Microsoft's liability was narrowed at the appellate level. When this case began with the filing of separate complaints by the Department and the plaintiff states in May of 1998, it was focused on Microsoft's integration of browsing functionality called Internet Explorer or IE into Windows 98, which the plaintiffs alleged to be an illegal tying arrangement.

The complaints of the Department and the states included five separate claims: (1) a claim under section 1 of the Sherman Act that the tie-in was per se illegal; (2) another claim under section I that certain promotion and distribution agreements with Internet service providers (ISPs), Internet content providers (ICPs), and on-line service providers (OSPs) constituted illegal exclusive dealing; (3) a claim under section 2 of the Sherman Act that Microsoft had attempted to monopolize Web browsing software; (4) a catch-all claim under section 2 that the alleged conduct that underlay the first three claims amounted to illegal maintenance of Microsoft's monopoly in PC operating systems; and (5) a claim by the plaintiff states (but not part of the Department's complaint) under section 2 that Microsoft illegally "leveraged" its monopoly in PC operating systems.[2] As discovery got underway, the case dramatically expanded as the plaintiffs indiscriminately began identifying all manner of Microsoft conduct as examples of the company's illegal efforts to maintain its monopoly. But then, the case began to shrink.

- In response to Microsoft's motion for summary judgment, the district court dismissed the states' Monopoly leveraging claim (claim 5).
- After trial, Judge Jackson held that the plaintiffs failed to prove that Microsoft's arrangements with ISPs, ICPs, and OSPs violated section 1 (claim 2).
- Judge Jackson did, however, conclude that the plaintiffs had sustained their claims that Microsoft illegally tied IE to Windows (claim 1), illegally attempted to monopolize the browser market (claim 3), and illegally maintained its monopoly (claim 4), basing his decision on 35 different actions engaged in by Microsoft.

[2] Initially the plaintiff states included an additional section 2 claim based on Microsoft Office; however, they voluntarily dropped that claim in their amended complaint.

- In a unanimous decision of the Court of Appeals sitting *en banc*, the court reversed the trial court on the attempted monopolization claim (claim 3) and remanded with instructions that judgment be entered on that claim in favor of Microsoft.
- The unanimous court also reversed Judge Jackson's decision with respect to the tie-in claim (claim 1). The appellate court held that, in light of the prospect of consumer benefit from integrating new functionality into platform software such as Windows, Microsoft's integration of IE into Windows had to be judged under the rule of reason rather than the per se approach taken by Judge Jackson. The Court of Appeals refused to apply the per se approach because of "our qualms about redefining the boundaries of a defendant's product and the possibility of consumer gains from simplifying the work of applications developers [by ensuring the ubiquitous dissemination of compatible APIs]." The court's decision did allow the plaintiffs on remand to pursue the tie-in claim on a rule of reason theory; however, shortly after the remand, the plaintiffs announced they were dropping the tie-in claim.
- With respect to the only remaining claim (monopoly maintenance—claim 4), the Court of Appeals affirmed in part and reversed in part the lower court and substantially shrank Microsoft's liability. After articulating a four-step burden-shifting test that is highly fact intensive, the appellate court reviewed the 35 different factual bases for liability and rejected nearly two-thirds of them.
  - In the case of seven of those 35 findings (concerning such conduct as Microsoft's refusal to allow OEMs to replace the Windows desktop, Microsoft's design of Windows to "override the user's choice of a default browser," and Microsoft's development of a Java virtual machine (JVM) that was incompatible with Sun's JVM), the appellate court specifically reversed Judge Jackson's decision.
  - The Court of Appeals dismissed sixteen of the remaining findings by reversing Judge Jackson's holding that Microsoft had engaged in a general "course of conduct" that amounted to illegal monopoly maintenance—the so-called "monopoly broth" theory.
  - With respect to the remaining twelve findings (concerning such things as Microsoft's refusal to allow PC manufacturers (OEMs) to remove end-user access to IE, Microsoft's exclusive arrangements with ISPs, and its "commingling" of software code to frustrate OEMs ability to hide access to IE), the court did affirm Judge Jackson's findings as not being "clearly erroneous." And even as to those twelve, a number were practices—for example, the arrangements with ISPs—that Microsoft had already ceased.

As a result, when the case was remanded to the district court and reassigned to Judge Kollar-Kotelly, four-fifths of the original claims were all but gone.[3] With respect to the sole surviving claim, nearly two-thirds of the supporting findings had been rejected by the Court of Appeals. In the words of the Court of Appeals, its decision "drastically altered the scope of Microsoft's liability."[4]

The Relevance of the Drastic Narrowing of Liability

The Court of Appeals' decision makes clear the critical significance of the drastic reduction in the scope of Microsoft's liability in terms of the relief to which the plaintiffs are entitled. As the court noted in instructing the lower court on how the remand for remedy should be handled,

> "A court . . . must base its relief on some clear 'indication of a significant causal connection between the conduct enjoined or mandated and the violation found directed toward the remedial goal intended.' 3 PHILLIP E. AREEDA & HERBERT HOVENKAMP, ANTITRUST LAW ¶ 653(b), at 91–92 (1996). In a case such as the one before us where sweeping equitable relief is employed to remedy multiple violations, and some—indeed most—of the findings of remedial violations do not withstand appellate scrutiny, it is necessary to vacate the remedy decree since the implicit findings of causal connection no longer exist to warrant our deferential affirmance. . . . *In particular, the [district] court*

---

[3] As indicated above, all that remained for the tie-in claim was the recognition by the plaintiffs that they could not establish the unreasonableness of Microsoft's integration of IE into Windows under the appellate court's rule of reason test. That recognition came when the Department informed Microsoft on September 6, that the plaintiffs would not be pursuing the tie-in claim on remand. At the same time, the plaintiffs informed the court that, in light of the Court of Appeals' decision, they would not be seeking divestiture.

[4] United States v. Microsoft, 253 F.3d 34, 105 (D.C.Cir. 2001).

should consider which of the decree's conduct restrictions remain viable in light of our modification of the original liability decision."[5]

At the time Judge Kollar-Kotelly ordered the parties into intensive negotiations, she clearly recognized the importance of the drastic alteration to the scope of Microsoft's liability.[6] The judge informed the government that its "first and most obvious task is going to be to determine which portions of the former judgment remain appropriate in light of the appellate court's ruling and which portions are unsupported following the appellate court's narrowing of liability."[7] The judge went on to note that "the scope of any proposed remedy must be carefully crafted so as to ensure that the enjoining conduct falls within the [penumbra] of behavior which was found to be anticompetitive."[8] The judge also stated that "Microsoft argues that some of the terms of the former judgment are no longer appropriate, and that is correct. I think there are certain portions where the liability has been narrowed."[9]

Before discussing the negotiations and the decree itself, I would like to make three other points about the crafting of antitrust remedies that also are relevant to considering the relief to which the plaintiffs were entitled. First, the critics of the PFJ routinely ignore the fact that the Department has long acknowledged that Microsoft lawfully acquired its monopoly position in PC operating systems. Indeed, the Department retained a Nobel laureate in the first Microsoft case in 1994 to submit an affidavit to the district court opining that Microsoft had reached its position in PC operating systems through luck, skill, and foresight.[10] It is true of course that Microsoft has now been found liable for engaging in conduct that amounted to illegal efforts to maintain that position; however, there is precious little in the record establishing any causal link between the twelve illegal acts of "monopoly maintenance" and Microsoft's current position in the market for PC operating systems. Thus, contrary to the critics' overheated rhetoric, there is no basis for relief designed to terminate an "illegal monopoly."

Second, decrees in civil antitrust cases are designed to remedy, not to punish. All too often, the critics of this decree speak as though Microsoft was convicted of a crime. It was not. This is a civil case, subject to the rules of civil rather than criminal procedure. To the extent the plaintiffs tried to get relief that could be deemed punitive, that relief would have been rejected.

Third, a decree must serve the purposes of the antitrust laws, which is a "consumer welfare prescription." I realize we are in the "season of giving," but an antitrust decree is not a Christmas tree to fulfill the wishes of competitors, particularly where that fulfillment comes at the expense of consumer welfare. Calls for royalty-free licensing of Microsoft's intellectual property, or for imposing obligations on Microsoft to distribute third party software at no charge, or for Microsoft to facilitate the distribution of an infinite variety of bastardized versions of Windows (and make sure they all run perfectly) are great for a small group of competitors who know that such provisions will quickly destroy Microsoft's incentives and ability to compete (not to mention violate the Constitution's proscription against "takings"). Such calls, however, are anathema to consumers' interests in a dynamic, innovative computer industry. Twenty years ago, my old boss and antitrust icon, Bill Baxter, warned about the anticompetitive consequences of antitrust decrees designed simply to "add sand to the saddlebags" of a particularly fleet competitor like Microsoft. It's a warning the courts would certainly heed today.

To their credit, the negotiators for the Department and the settling states understood these three fundamental antitrust principles. While we may have had to remind the other side of these principles from time to time, we did not have to negotiate for their adherence to them. Taxpayers and consumers can be proud that their interests were represented by honorable men and women with the utmost respect for the rule of law. For others to insinuate that, by agreeing to a decree that honors these three fundamental principles, the Department and the settling states "caved" or settled for inadequate relief is as offensive as it is laughable.

---

[5] *Id.* (emphasis added).

[6] This hearing, it should be noted, occurred after the plaintiffs had dropped their request for divestiture relief.

[7] Transcript of Scheduling Conference before the Honorable Colleen Kollar-Kotelly, September 28, 2001, at 8.

[8] *Id.*

[9] *Id.*

[10] The Declaration of Kenneth J. Arrow was attached as an exhibit to the Memorandum of the United States in Support of Motion to Enter Final Judgment, filed on January 18, 1995, with the District Court in support of the Department's 1994 consent decree with Microsoft.

The Negotiations

It is against the background I have sketched that, on September 27th, Judge KollarKotelly ordered the parties into intensive, "around the clock" negotiations. Microsoft had already indicated publicly its strong desire to try to settle the case, and so it welcomed the judge's order. As has been widely reported, all the parties in the case took the court's order very seriously. Microsoft assembled in Washington, D.C., a core team of in-house and outside lawyers who have been living with this case for years, and who spent virtually all of the next five weeks camped out in my offices down the street. Microsoft's top legal officer was in town during much of the period directing the negotiations. Back in Redmond, the company's most senior executives devoted a great deal of time and energy to the process, and we were all supported by a large group of dedicated lawyers, businesspeople, and staff.

From my vantage point, the Department and the states (at least those that settled) made an equivalent effort. As the mediator wrote after the process ended, "No party was left out of the negotiations. . . . Throughout most of the mediation the 19 states (through their executive Committee representatives) and the federal government (through the staff of the antitrust division) worked as a combined 'plaintiffs' team."[11] Jay Himes from the office of the New York Attorney General Eliot Spitzer and Beth Finnerty from the office of the Ohio Attorney General Betty Montgomery represented the states throughout the negotiations, putting in the same long hours as the rest of us. At various points Mr. Himes and Ms. Finnerty were joined by representatives from other states, including Kevin O'Connor from the office of Wisconsin Attorney General James Doyle.[12]

The negotiations began on September 28th and continued virtually non-stop until November 6th. During the first two weeks, we negotiated without the benefit of a mediator. As they say in diplomatic circles, the discussions were "full and frank." The Department lawyers and the state representatives in the negotiation were extremely knowledgeable, diligent, and formidable.

Microsoft certainly hoped to be able to reach a settlement quickly and before a mediator was designated. However, the views on all sides were sufficiently strong and the need to pay attention to every sentence, phrase, and punctuation mark so overwhelming that reaching agreement proved impossible in those first two weeks. Eric Green, a prominent mediation specialist, was appointed by the court and with the help of Jonathan Marks spent the next three weeks helping the parties find common ground. As Professor Green and Mr. Marks wrote after the mediation ended, "Successful mediations are ones in which mediators and parties work to identify and overcome barriers to reaching agreement. Successful mediations are ones in which all the parties engage in reasoned discussions of issues that divide them, of options for settlement, and of the risks, opportunities, and costs that each party faces if a settlement isn't reached. Successful mediations are ones in which, settle or not, senior representatives of each party have made informed and intelligent decisions. The Microsoft mediation was successful."[13]

Working day and night virtually until the original November 2 deadline set by the judge, Microsoft and the Department agreed to and signed a decree early on November 2. The representatives of the states also tentatively agreed, subject to an opportunity from November 2 until November 6 to confer with the other states that were more removed from the case and negotiations. During that period, the states requested several clarifying modifications to which Microsoft (and the Department) agreed. From press reports, it appears that during this period the plaintiff states also were being subjected to intense lobbying by a few of Microsoft's competitors who were desperate either to get a decree that would severely cripple if not eventually destroy Microsoft or at least to keep the litigation (and the attendant costs imposed on Microsoft) going. Notwithstanding that pressure, New York, Wisconsin, and Ohio—the states that had made the largest investment in litigating against Microsoft and in negotiating a settlement—along with six other plaintiff states represented by a bipartisan group of state attorneys general signed onto the Revised PFJ on November 6.

The Proposed Final Judgment

Throughout the negotiations, Microsoft was confronted by a determined and tough group of negotiators for the Department and the states. They made clear that there would be no settlement unless Microsoft went well beyond the relief to which, Micro-

---

[11] Eric D. Green and Jonathan B. Marks, How We Mediated the Microsoft Case, Boston Globe, at A23 (November 15, 2001).

[12] Mr. O'Connor, as well as attorneys in the office of the New York Attorney General, had served as counsel of record for the states in the litigation.

[13] Green and Marks, *supra* fn. 11.

soft believes, the Court of Appeals opinion and the law entitles the plaintiffs. Once that became clear, Microsoft relented in significant ways, subject only to narrow language that preserved Microsoft's ability to innovate and engage in normal, clearly procompetitive activities. Professor Green, the one neutral observer of this drama, has noted the broad scope of the prohibitions and obligations imposed on Microsoft by the PFJ, stating during the status conference with Judge Kollar-Kotelly that "the parties have not stopped at the outer limits of the Court of Appeals' decision, but in some important respects the proposed final judgment goes beyond the issues affirmed by the Court of Appeals to deal with issues important to the parties in this rapidly-changing technology."[14]

I do not intend today to provide a detailed description of each provision of the PFJ; the provisions speak for themselves. It may come as something of a surprise in light of some of the uninformed criticism hurled at the decree, but one of Microsoft's principal objectives during the negotiations was to develop proscriptions and obligations that were sufficiently clear, precise and certain to ensure that the company and its employees would be able to understand and comply with the decree without constantly engendering disputes with the Department. This is an area of complex technology and the decree terms on which the Department insisted entailed a degree of technical sophistication that is unprecedented in an antitrust decree. Drafting to these specifications was not easy, but the resulting PFJ is infinitely clearer and easier to administer than the conduct provisions of the decree that Judge Jackson imposed in June 2000.

If, as one might suspect would be the outcome in a case such as this, the PFJ were written to proscribe only the twelve practices affirmed by the Court of Appeals, the decree would be much shorter and simpler. The Department and settling states, however, insisted that the decree go beyond just focused prohibitions to create much more general protections for a potentially large category of software, which the PFJ calls "middleware." But even these expansive provisions to foster middleware competition were not sufficient to induce the Department and the states to settle; rather, they insisted that Microsoft also agree to additional obligations that bear virtually no relationship to any of the issues addressed by the district court and the Court of Appeals. And lastly they insisted on unprecedented enforcement provisions. I will briefly describe each of these three sets of provisions.

1. Protections for "Middleware"

The case that the plaintiffs tried and the narrowed liability that survived appellate review all hinged on claims that Microsoft took certain actions to exclude Netscape's Navigator browser and Sun's Java technology from the market in order to protect the Windows operating system monopoly. The plaintiffs successfully argued that Microsoft feared that Navigator and Java, either alone or together, might eventually include and expose a broad set of general purpose APIs to which software developers could write as an alternative to the Windows APIs. Since Navigator and Java can run on multiple operating systems, if they developed into general purpose platforms, Navigator and Java would provide a means of overcoming the "applications barrier" to entry and threaten the position of the Windows operating system as platform software.

A person might expect that a decree designed to address such a monopoly maintenance claim would provide relief with respect to Web-browsing software and Java or, at most, to other general purpose platform software that exposes a broad set of APIs and is ported to run on multiple operating systems. The PFJ goes much further. The Department insisted that obligations imposed on Microsoft by the decree extend to a range of software that has little in common with Navigator and Java. The decree applies to "middleware" broadly defined to include, in addition to Web-browsing software and Java, instant messaging software, media players, and even email clients—software that, Microsoft believes, has virtually no chance of developing into broad, general purpose platforms that might threaten to displace the Windows platform. In addition, there is a broad catch-all definition of middleware that in the future is likely to sweep other similar software into the decree.

This sweeping definition of middleware is significant because of the substantial obligations it imposes on Microsoft. Those obligations—a number of which lack any correspondence to the monopoly maintenance findings that survived appellate review—are intended to create protections for all the vendors of software that fits within the middleware definition. Taken together, the decree provisions provide the following protections and opportunities:

---

[14] Transcript of Status Conference before the Honorable Colleen Kollar-Kotelly, November 2, 2001, at 5.

- *Relations with Computer Makers*. Microsoft has agreed not to retaliate against computer makers who ship software that competes with anything in its Windows operating system.
- *Computer Maker Flexibility*. Microsoft has agreed to grant computer makers broad new rights to configure Windows so as to promote non-Microsoft software programs that compete with features of Windows. Computer makers will now be free to remove the means by which consumers access important features of Windows, such as Internet Explorer, Windows Media Player, and Windows Messenger. Notwithstanding the billions of dollars Microsoft invests developing such cool new features, computer makers will now be able to replace access to them in order to give prominence to non-Microsoft software such as programs from AOL Time Warner or RealNetworks. (Additionally, as is the case today, computer makers can provide consumers with a choice—that is to say access to Windows features as well as to non-Microsoft software programs.)
- *Windows Design Obligations*. Microsoft has agreed to design future versions of Windows, beginning with an interim release of Windows XP, to provide a mechanism to make it easy for computer makers, consumers and software developers to promote nonMicrosoft software within Windows. The mechanism will make it easy to add or remove access to features built in to Windows or to non-Microsoft software. Consumers will have the freedom to choose to change their configuration at any time.
- *Internal Interface Disclosure*. Even though there is no suggestion in the Court of Appeals' decision that Microsoft fails to disclose APIs today and even though the Court of Appeals' holding on monopoly power is predicated on the idea that there are tens of thousands of applications written to call upon those APIs, Microsoft has agreed to document and disclose for use by its competitors various interfaces that are internal to Windows operating system products.
- *Relations with Software Developers*. Microsoft has agreed not to retaliate against software or hardware developers who develop or promote software that competes with Windows or that runs on software that competes with Windows.
- *Contractual Restrictions*. Microsoft has agreed not to enter into any agreements obligating any third party to distribute or promote any Windows technology exclusively or in a fixed percentage, subject to certain narrow exceptions that apply to agreements raising no competitive concern. Microsoft has also agreed not to enter into agreements relating to Windows that obligate any software developer to refrain from developing or promoting software that competes with Windows.

These obligations go far beyond the twelve practices that the Court of Appeals found to constitute monopoly maintenance. One of the starkest examples of the extent to which these provisions go beyond the Court of Appeals decision relates to Microsoft's obligations to design Windows in such a way as to give third parties the ability to designate non-Microsoft middleware as the "default" choice in certain circumstances in which Windows might otherwise be designed to utilize functionality integrated into Windows. As support for his monopoly maintenance conclusion, Judge Jackson had relied on several circumstances in which Windows was designed to override the end users' choice of Navigator as their default browser and instead to invoke IE. The Court of Appeals, however, reviewed those circumstances and reversed Judge Jackson's conclusion on the ground that Microsoft had "valid technical reasons" for designing Windows as it did. Notwithstanding this clear victory, Microsoft acceded to the Department's demands that it design future versions of Windows to ensure certain default opportunities for non-Microsoft middleware.

2. Uniform Prices and Server Interoperability

Nevertheless, agreeing to this wide range of prohibitions and obligations designed to encourage the development of middleware broadly defined was not enough to get the plaintiffs to settle. Instead, they insisted on two additional substantive provisions that have absolutely no correspondence to the findings of monopoly maintenance liability that survived appeal.

- *Uniform Price List*. Microsoft has agreed to license its Windows operating system products to the 20 largest computer makers (who collectively account for the great majority of PC sales) on identical terms and conditions, including price (subject to reasonable volume discounts for computer makers who ship large volumes of Windows).
- *Client/Server Interoperability*. Microsoft has agreed to make available to its competitors, on reasonable and non-discriminatory terms, any protocols implemented in Windows desktop operating systems that are used to interoperate natively with any Microsoft server operating system.

In the case of the sweeping definition of middleware and the range of prohibitions and obligations imposed on Microsoft, there is at least a patina of credibility to the argument that the penumbra of the twelve monopoly maintenance practices affirmed by the Court of Appeals can be stretched to justify those provisions, at least as "fencing in" provisions. There is no sensible reading of the Court of Appeals decision that would provide any basis for requiring Microsoft to charge PC manufacturers uniform prices or to make available the proprietary protocols used by Windows desktop operating systems and Windows server operating systems to communicate with each other. Nevertheless, because the plaintiffs insisted that they would not settle without those two provisions, Microsoft also agreed to them.

Before turning to the enforcement provisions of the PFJ, I want to say a word about the few provisos included in the decree that provide narrow exceptions to the various prohibitions and obligations imposed on Microsoft. Those exceptions were critical to Microsoft's willingness to agree to the sweeping provisions on which the plaintiffs insisted. Without these narrowly tailored exceptions, Microsoft could not innovate or engage in normal procompetitive commercial activities. The public can rest assured that the settling plaintiffs insisted on language to ensure that the exceptions only apply when they promote consumer welfare. For example, some companies that compete with Microsoft for the sale of server operating systems apparently have complained about the so-called "security carve-out" to Microsoft's obligation to disclose internal interfaces and protocols. That exception is very narrow and only allows Microsoft to withhold encryption "keys" and the similar mechanisms that must be kept secret if the security of computer networks and the privacy of user information is to be ensured. In light of all the concern over computer privacy and security these days, it is surprising that there is any controversy over such a narrow exception.

3. Compliance and Enforcement

The broad substantive provisions of the PFJ are complemented by an unusually strong set of compliance and enforcement provisions. Those provisions are unprecedented in a civil antitrust decree. The PFJ creates an independent three-person technical Committee, resident on the Microsoft campus, with extraordinary powers and full access to Microsoft facilities, records, employees and proprietary technical data, including Windows source code, which is the equivalent of the "secret formula" for Coke. The technical Committee provides a level of technical oversight that is far more substantial than any provision of any other antitrust decree of which I am aware. At the insistence of the plaintiffs, the technical Committee does not have independent enforcement authority; rather, reports to the plaintiffs and, through them, to the court. The investigative and oversight authority of the technical Committee in no way limits or reduces the enforcement powers of the DOJ and states; rather, the technical Committee supplements and enhances those powers. Each of the settling states and DOJ have the power to enforce the decree and have the ability to monitor compliance and seek a broad range of remedies in the event of a violation.

Microsoft also agreed to develop and implement an internal antitrust compliance program, to distribute the decree and educate its management and employees as to the various restrictions and obligations. In recent years, Microsoft has assembled in-house one of the largest, most talented groups of antitrust lawyers in corporate America. They are already engaged in substantial antitrust compliance counseling and monitoring. The decree formalizes those efforts, and quite frankly adds very substantially to the in-house lawyers' work. As we speak, that group, together with key officials from throughout the Microsoft organization, are working to implement the decree and to ensure the company's compliance with it.

As with the substantive provisions, Microsoft agreed to these unprecedented compliance and enforcement provisions because of the adamance of the plaintiffs and because of the highly technical nature of the decree. Microsoft, the Department, and the settling states recognized that it was appropriate to include mechanisms—principally, the technical Committee—that will facilitate the prompt and expert resolution of any technical disputes that might be raised by third parties, without in any way derogating from the government's full enforcement powers under the decree. Although the enforcement provisions are unprecedented in their stringency and scope, they are not necessitated or justified by any valid claim that Microsoft has failed to comply with its decree obligations in the past. In fact, Microsoft has an exemplary record of complying with the consent decree to which the company and the Department agreed in 1994. In 1997, the Department did question whether Microsoft's integration of IE into Windows 95 violated a "fencing in" provision that prohibited contractual tie-ins, but Microsoft was ultimately vindicated by the Court of Appeals.[15] Microsoft has committed itself to that same level of dedication in ensuring the company's compliance with the PFJ.

Conclusion

The PFJ strikes an appropriate balance in this complicated case, providing opportunities and protections for firms seeking to compete while allowing Microsoft to continue to innovate and bring new technologies to market. The decree is faithful to the fact that the antitrust laws are a "consumer protection prescription," and it ensures an economic environment in which all parts of the PC-ecosystem can thrive.

Make no mistake, however, the PFJ is tough. It will impose substantial new obligations on the company, and it will require significant changes in the way Microsoft does business. It imposes heavy costs on the company and entails a degree of oversight that is unprecedented in a civil antitrust case. For some competitors of Microsoft, however, apparently nothing short of the destruction of Microsoft—or at least the ongoing distraction of litigation—will be sufficient. But if the objective is to protect the interests of consumers and the competitiveness process, then this decree more than achieves that goal.

Finally, for all those who are worried about the future and what unforeseen developments may not be covered by this case and the decree, remember that the Court of Appeals decision now provides guideposts, which previously did not exist, for judging Microsoft's behavior, and that of other high technology companies, going forward. Those guidelines, it is true, are not always easy to apply *ex ante* to conduct; however, now that the Court of Appeals has spoken, we all have a much better idea of the way in which section 2 of the Sherman Act applies to the software industry. In short, what antitrust law requires of Microsoft is today much clearer than it was when this case began. We have all learned a lot over the last four years, and Microsoft has every incentive to ensure that history does not repeat itself.

---

[15] United States v. Microsoft, 147 F.3d 935 (D.C.Cir. 1998).

The Court of Appeals' Roadmap for Relief

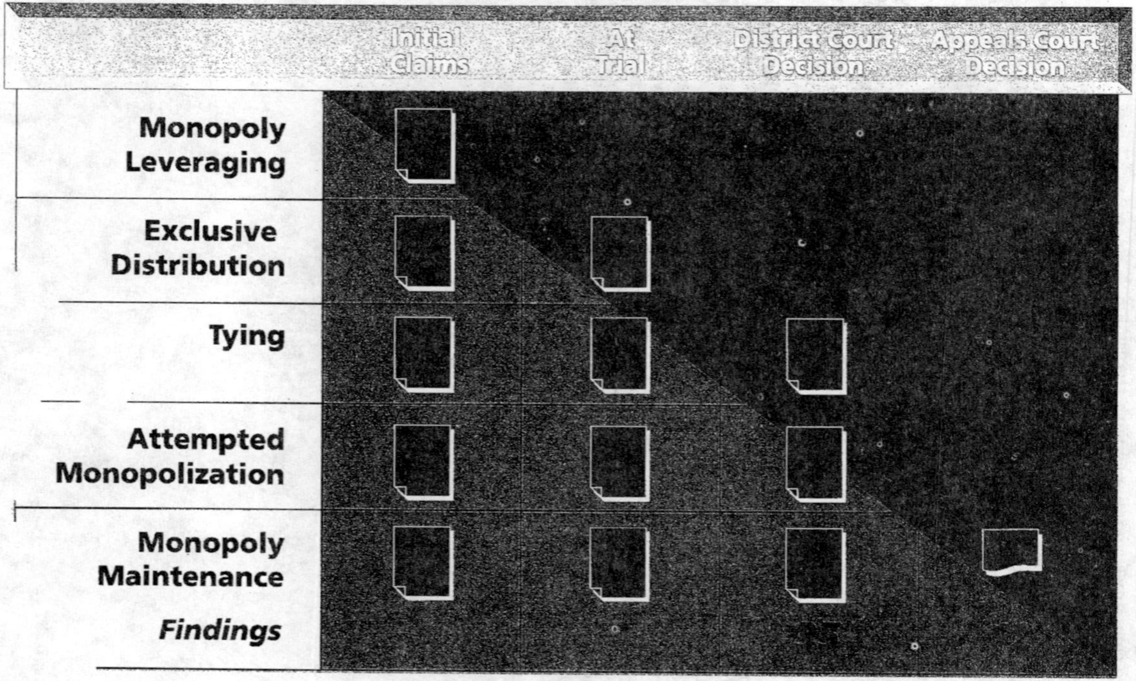

Ralph Nader
P.O. Box 19312
Washington, DC 20036

December 11, 2001

Senator Patrick Leahy
Judiciary Committee
US Senate
Washington, DC

Via fax: 1.202.224.9516

Dear Senator Leahy:

This is a quick note to express my disappointment that I will not be among the panel members for the December 12, 2001 hearing on Microsoft. James Love on our staff made a number of telephone calls to your Judiciary Committee staff asking that he or I be permitted to testify, beginning as soon as the hearings were first announced. As you may know, we played an instrumental role in 1997 in pushing the Department of Justice to bring this antitrust case, and hosted two key conferences that helped frame the discussions over the case and the proposed remedies (http://www.appraising-microsoft.org). I am attaching also two letters James Love and I have recently sent regarding the government and private antitrust cases. Would you please include these letters in the printed hearing record. Thank you.

Sincerely,

Ralph Nader

Ralph Nader
P.O. Box 19312
Washington, DC 20036

James Love
Consumer Project on Technology
P.O. Box 19367
Washington, DC 20036

November 5, 2001

Judge Colleen Kollar-Kotelly
United States District Court for the District of Columbia
333 Constitution Avenue, NW
Washington, DC 20001

RE: US v. Microsoft proposed final order

Dear Judge Kollar-Kotelly,

Introduction

Having examined the proposed consent final judgment for USA versus Microsoft, we offer the following initial comments. We note at the outset that the decision to push for a rapid negotiation appears to have placed the Department of Justice at a disadvantage, given Microsoft's apparently willingness to let this matter drag on for years, through different USDOJ antitrust chiefs, Presidents and judges. The proposal is obviously limited in terms of effectiveness by the desire to obtain a final order that is agreeable to Microsoft.

We are disappointed of course that the court has moved away from a **structural** remedy, which we believe would require less dependence upon future enforcement efforts and good faith by Microsoft, and which would jump start a more competitive market for applications. Within the limits of a **conduct-only** remedy, we make the following observations.

On the positive side, we find the proposed final order addresses important areas where Microsoft has abused its monopoly power, particularly in terms of its OEM licensing practices and on the issue of using interoperability as a weapon against consumers of non-Microsoft products. There are, however, important areas where the interoperability remedies should be stronger. For example, there is a need to have broader disclosure of **file formats** for popular office productivity and multimedia applications. Moreover, where Microsoft appears be given broad discretion to deploy intellectual property claims to avoid opening up its monopoly operating system where it will be needed the most, in terms of new interfaces and technologies. Moreover, the agreement appears to give Microsoft too many opportunities to undermine the free software movement.

We also find the agreement wanting in several other areas.. It is astonishing that the agreement fails to provide any penalty for Microsoft's past misdeeds, creating both the sense that Microsoft is escaping punishment because of its extraordinary political and economic power, and undermining the value of antitrust penalties as a deterrent. Second, the agreement does not adequately address the concerns about Microsoft's failure to abide by the spirit or the letter of previous agreements, offering a weak oversight regime that suffers in several specific areas. Indeed, the proposed alternative dispute resolution for compliance with the agreement embraces many of the worst features of such systems, operating in secrecy, lacking independence, and open to undue influence from Microsoft.

OEM Licensing Remedies

We were pleased that the proposed final order provides for non-discriminatory licensing of Windows to OEMs, and that these remedies include multiple boot PCs, substitution of non-Microsoft middleware, changes in the management of visible icons and other issues. These remedies would have been more effective if they would have been extended to Microsoft Office, the other key component of Microsoft's monopoly power in the PC client software market, and if they permitted the removal of Microsoft products. But nonetheless, they are pro-competitive, and do represent real benefits to consumers.

Interoperability Remedies

Microsoft regularly punishes consumers who buy non-Microsoft products, or who fail to upgrade and repurchase newer versions of Microsoft products, by designing Microsoft Windows or Office products to be incompatible or non-interoperable with competitor software, or even older versions of its own software. It is therefore good that the proposed final order would require Microsoft to address a wide range of interoperability remedies, including for example the disclosures of APIs for Windows and Microsoft middleware products, non-discriminatory access to communications protocols used for services, and non-discriminatory licensing of certain intellectual property rights for Microsoft middleware products. There are, however, many areas where these remedies may be limited by Microsoft, and as is indicated by the record in this case, Microsoft can and does take advantage of any loopholes in contracts to create barriers to competition and enhance and extend its monopoly power.

Special Concerns for Free Software Movement

The provisions in J.1 and J.2. appear to give Microsoft too much flexibility in withholding information on security grounds, and to provide Microsoft with the power to set unrealistic burdens on a rival's legitimate rights to obtain interoperability data. More generally, the provisions in D. regarding the sharing of technical information permit

Microsoft to choose secrecy and limited disclosures over more openness. In particular, these clauses and others in the agreement do not reflect an appreciation for the importance of new software development models, including those "open source" or "free" software development models which are now widely recognized as providing an important safeguard against Microsoft monopoly power, and upon which the Internet depends.

The overall acceptance of Microsoft's limits on the sharing of technical information to the broader public is an important and in our view core flaw in the proposed agreement. The agreement should require that this information be as freely available as possible, with a high burden on Microsoft to justify secrecy. Indeed, there is ample evidence that Microsoft is focused on strategies to cripple the free software movement, which it publicly considers an important competitive threat. This is particularly true for software developed under the GNU Public License (GPL), which is used in GNU/Linux, the most important rival to Microsoft in the server market. Consider, for example, comments earlier this year by Microsoft executive Jim Allchin:

> http://news.cnet.com/news/0-1003-200-4833927.html
>
> "Microsoft exec calls open source a threat to innovation," Bloomberg News, February 15, 2001, 11:00 a.m. PT
>
> One of Microsoft's high-level executives says that freely distributed software code such as Linux could stifle innovation and that legislators need to understand the threat.
>
> The result will be the demise of both intellectual property rights and the incentive to spend on research and development, Microsoft Windows operating-system chief Jim Allchin said this week
>
> Microsoft has told U.S. lawmakers of its concern while discussing protection of intellectual property rights . . .
>
> "Open source is an intellectual-property destroyer," Allchin said. "I can't imagine something that could be worse than this for the software business and the intellectual-property business."

In a June 1, 2001 interview with the Chicago Sun Times, Microsoft CEO Steve Ballmer again complained about the GNU/Linux business model, saying "Linux is a cancer that attaches itself in an intellectual property sense to everything it touches. That's the way that the license works,"[1] leading to a round of new stories, including for example this account in CNET.Com:

[1] http://www.suntimes.com/output/tech/cst-fin-micro01.html "Microsoft CEO takes launch break with the Sun-Times," Chicago Sun Times, June 1, 2001.

http://news.cnet.com/news/0-1003-200-6291224.html

"Why Microsoft is wary of open source: Joe Wilcox and Stephen Shankland in CNET.com, June 18, 2001.

There's more to Microsoft's recent attacks on the open-source movement than mere rhetoric: Linux's popularity could hinder the software giant in its quest to gain control of a server market that's crucial to its long-term goals

Recent public statements by Microsoft executives have cast Linux and the open-source philosophy that underlies it as, at the minimum, bad for competition, and, at worst, a "cancer" to everything it touches.
Behind the war of words, analysts say, is evidence that Microsoft is increasingly concerned about Linux and its growing popularity. The Unix-like operating system "has clearly emerged as the spoiler that will prevent Microsoft from achieving a dominant position" in the worldwide server operating-system market, IDC analyst Al Gillen concludes in a forthcoming report.

. . . While Linux hasn't displaced Windows, it has made serious inroads. . .]. . In attacking Linux and open source, Microsoft finds itself competing "not against another company, but against a grassroots movement," said Paul Dain, director of application development at Emeryville, Calif.-based Wirestone, a technology services company.

. . . Microsoft has also criticized the General Public License (GPL) that governs the heart of Linux. Under this license, changes to the Linux core, or kernel, must also be governed by the GPL. The license means that if a company changes the kernel, it must publish the changes and can't keep them proprietary if it plans to distribute the code externally. . .

Microsoft's open-source attacks come at a time when the company has been putting the pricing squeeze on customers. In early May, Microsoft revamped software licensing, raising upgrades between 33 percent and 107 percent, according to Gartner. A large percentage of Microsoft business customers could in fact be compelled to upgrade to Office XP before Oct. 1 or pay a heftier purchase price later on.

The action "will encourage--'force' may be a more accurate term--customers to upgrade much sooner than they had otherwise planned," Gillen noted in the IDC report. "Once the honeymoon period runs out in October 2001, the only way to 'upgrade' from a product that is not considered to be current technology is to buy a brand-new full license.'"

> This could make open-source Linux's GPL more attractive to some customers feeling trapped by the price hike, Gillen said. "Offering this form of 'upgrade protection' may motivate some users to seriously consider alternatives to Microsoft technology." . . .

What is surprising is that the US Department of Justice allowed Microsoft to place so many provisions in the agreement that can be used to undermine the free software movement. Note for example that under J.1 and J.2 of the proposed final order, Microsoft can withhold technical information from third parties on the grounds that Microsoft does not certify the "authenticity and viability of its business," while at the same time it is describing the licensing system for Linux as a "cancer" that threatens the demise of both the intellectual property rights system and the future of research and development.

The agreement provides Microsoft with a rich set of strategies to undermine the development of free software, which depends upon the free sharing of technical information with the general public, taking advantage of the collective intelligence of users of software, who share ideas on improvements in the code. If Microsoft can tightly control access to technical information under a court approved plan, or charge fees, and use its monopoly power over the client space to migrate users to proprietary interfaces, it will harm the development of key alternatives, and lead to a less contestable and less competitive platform, with more consumer lock-in, and more consumer harm, as Microsoft continues to hike up its prices for its monopoly products.

Problems with the term and the enforcement mechanism

Another core concern with the proposed final order concerns the term of the agreement and the enforcement mechanisms. We believe a five-to-seven year term is artificially brief, considering that this case has already been litigated in one form or another since 1994, and the fact that Microsoft's dominance in the client OS market is stronger today than it has ever been, and it has yet to face a significant competitive threat in the client OS market. An artificial end will give Microsoft yet another incentive to delay, meeting each new problem with an endless round of evasions and creative methods of circumventing the pro-competitive aspects of the agreement. Only if Microsoft believes it will have to come to terms with its obligations will it modifv its strategy of anticompetitive abuses.

Even within the brief period of the term of the agreement, Microsoft has too much room to co-opt the enforcement effort. Microsoft, despite having been found to be a law breaker by the courts, is given the right to select one member of the three members of the Technical Committee, who in turn gets a voice in selecting the third member. The committee is gagged, and sworn to secrecy, denying the public any information on Microsoft's compliance with the agreement, and will be paid by Microsoft, working inside Microsoft's headquarters. The public won't know if this committee spends its time playing golf with Microsoft executives, or investigating Microsoft's anticompetitive activities. Its ability to interview Microsoft employees will be extremely limited by the provisions that give Microsoft the opportunity to insist on having its lawyers present. One would be hard pressed to imagine an enforcement mechanism that would do less to make Microsoft accountable, which is probably why Microsoft has accepted its terms of reference.

In its 1984 agreement with the European Commission, IBM was required to affirmatively resolve compatibility issues raised by its competitors, and the EC staff had annual meetings with IBM to review its progress in resolve disputes. The EC reserved the right to revisit its enforcement action on IBM if it was not satisfied with IBM's conduct.

The court could require that the Department of Justice itself or some truly independent parties appoint the members of the TC, and give the TC real investigative powers, take them off Microsoft's payroll, and give them staff and the authority to inform the public of progress in resolving compliance problems, including for example an annual report that could include information on past complaints, as well as suggestions for modifications of the order that may be warranted by Microsoft's conduct. The TC could be given real enforcement powers, such as the power to levy fines on Microsoft. The level of fines that would serve as a deterrent for cash rich Microsoft would be difficult to fathom, but one might make these fines deter more by directing the money to be paid into trust funds that would fund the development of free software, an endeavor that Microsoft has indicated it strongly opposes as a threat to its own monopoly. This would give Microsoft a much greater incentive to abide by the agreement.

Failure to address Ill Gotten Gains

Completely missing from the proposed final order is anything that would make Microsoft pay for its past misdeeds, and this is an omission that must be remedied. Microsoft is hardly a first time offender, and has never shown remorse for its conduct, choosing instead to repeatedly attack the motives and character of officers of the government and members of the judiciary.

Microsoft has profited richly from the maintenance of its monopoly. On September 30, 2001, Microsoft reported cash and short-term investments of $36.2 billion, up from $31.6 billion the previous quarter -- an accumulation of more than $1.5 billion **per month**.

It is astounding that Microsoft would face only a "sin no more" edict from a court, after its long and tortured history of evasion of antitrust enforcement and its extraordinary embrace of anticompetitive practices -- practices recognized as illegal by all members of the DC Circuit court. The court has a wide range of options that would address the most egregious of Microsoft's past misdeeds. For example, even if the court decided to forgo the break-up of the Windows and Office parts of the company, it could require more targeted divestitures, such as divestitures of its browser technology and media player technologies, denying Microsoft the fruits of its illegal conduct, and it could require affirmative support for rival middleware products that it illegally acted to sabotage. Instead the proposed order permits Microsoft to consolidate the benefits from past misdeeds, while preparing for a weak oversight body tasked with monitoring future misdeeds only. What kind of a signal does this send to the public and to other large corporate law breakers? That economic crimes pay!

Please consider these and other criticisms of the settlement proposal, and avoid if possible yet another weak ending to a Microsoft antitrust case. Better to send this unchastened monopoly juggernaut a sterner message.

Sincerely,

Ralph Nader James Love

Cc: Stanley Sporkin, Judge Thomas Penfield Jackson, Anne K. Bingaman. Joel I. Klein

Ralph Nader
P.O. Box 19312
Washington, DC 20036

James Love
Consumer Project on Technology
P.O. Box 19367
Washington, DC 20036

December 10, 2001

Judge Honorable J. Frederick Motz
United States District Court
District of Maryland
101 West Lombard Street
Room 510
Baltimore, MD 21201

Fax: +1.410.962.2698

RE: Microsoft Corp. Antitrust Litigation, MDL No. 1332

Dear Judge Motz:

We are writing to ask that you reject the proposed settlement to the private antitrust actions against Microsoft, on the grounds that the settlement is inadequate in terms of the relief, anticompetitive in terms of its structure, and is among the least effective mechanisms for expanding access to educational services.

Microsoft has extraordinary global monopoly power in several essential software markets, including most notably its more than 90 percent market share for the operating systems (Windows), word processing (Word), spreadsheets (Excel) and presentation graphics (Powerpoint), and it has engaged in the equivalent of an antitrust crime spree, using an astonishing array of anticompetitive practices to consolidate and expand its monopoly power. As a consequence, consumers are denied the benefits of competition, and suffer from sluggish innovation, poor quality products, fewer choices, and high prices.

The Microsoft monopoly is highly profitable, and allowed Microsoft to accumulate an astonishing $1.5 billion per month in cash last quarter. The proposed settlement of the private antitrust claim is not only a tiny sum in comparison to

Microsoft's sales ($1 billion every 13 days currently), but it will not even be paid in cash. It isn't as if Microsoft can't afford to pay. It has cash reserves more than $36 billion right now. Microsoft simply sees the resolution of this antitrust case as a great opportunity to engage in more anticompetitive conduct -- in this case converting its liabilities for antitrust damages into a slush fund to undermine its competitors in the educational market.

The court should not allow the lawyers who have proposed this settlement to bury this important antitrust case with yet another disappointment in the long history of weak efforts to reign in Microsoft's assaults on consumers. The settlement should not be yet another marketing effort by Microsoft aimed at the strategically important education market. It should provide a measure of justice that has yet eluded a long list of law enforcement officials.

We object to many aspects of the settlement.

* The size of the damages is small by any reasonable interpretation of the harm to consumers.

* Microsoft is demonstrating zero remorse for its price gouging, and indeed has engaged in its most aggressive price hikes to date, as it continues to narrow consumer rights in license agreements, raises standard and negotiated license fees (including those for the educational market), and steps up its coercive strategies to force upgrades, such as its abandonment of support for older licenses, and the introduction of new non-interoperable technologies that will not work without increasingly frequent upgrades.

* The proposal will make it even less attractive for schools to purchase products from Microsoft competitors, because Microsoft will subsidize its sales from the antitrust settlement costs, having the intended and entirely predictable effect of strengthening Microsoft's marketshare and weakening further its few remaining rivals. Moreover, to the degree that the funds from the settlement are small relative to the number of schools that will seek grants or donations, and if Microsoft is perceived to play any role in determining who obtains grants, schools may be reluctant to purchase products from Microsoft rivals, thinking this will undermine their chances of receiving benefits from the settlement fund, allowing Microsoft to leverage the anticompetitive effect of the settlement fund. (One need only look at the comments filed in this proceeding to appreciate how eager various non-profit institutions are to curry favor with Microsoft. Many groups that have received Microsoft grants are now on record opposing efforts to reject this settlement as inadequate and anticompetitive.) For schools, the more important issue is dealing with skyrocketing license fees, which this settlement will only address in a minor way, for a small number of users, and for only a short time.

If the court wishes to direct the settlement resources for the educational market, it should do so in such a way as to promote competition, rather than to reduce competition. One solution would be to place the money into a trust fund to be used only for purchases of non-Microsoft products, creating a needed boost to the market for alternatives. Another would be to require the funds be donated to groups who develop free software alternatives -- these very alternatives that Microsoft executives have claimed were their main competitive threat during the USDOJ/State AG antitrust litigation. Either of these approaches will directly address the longer term concern over software pricing, the problem this case seeks to remedy.

Sincerely,

Ralph Nader

James Love
Consumer Project on Technology

Statement of Matthew J. Szulik, President and CEO, Red Hat, Inc., Durham, North Carolina

Good morning.

I would like to thank the members of the Committee for allowing me to contribute my views on a topic that I feel is of vital importance to the future of our nation. I stand before you today as Winston Churchill said, "only to fight while there is a chance, so we don't have to fight when there is non." Through your actions, members of the Committee can affect a remedy that many members of the growing, global technical community hope will restore balance and inspire competitiveness in a networked society free of monopolistic practices.

I stand before you today as a representative of the open source community. And as the CEO of Red Hat, Inc., generally regarded as the most successful company that sells and supports open source software. The Red Hat Linux operating system software we sell is created by a global community of volunteers. Volunteers who share their creation of intellectual property. The basis for their work is an open license that requires improvements to the technology be shared with others. Programmers submit their software code, their creations to the scrutiny of a very critical community of peers. The best code wins and is included in the next version of the software. This open communication strikes me as so perfectly American. I envision the early leaders of this country drawing up the tenets of our constitution in much the same way—in the open, in pursuit of a solution that is fair and of benefit to all.

Some have called this the technology equivalent of a barn-raising. Through this approach Linux software has grown, improved and become one of the most stable, cost-effective operating systems in the world. It continues to improve every day.

The values and practices of Red Hat are in most ways antithetical to those of the monopolist I am here to reference.

Much testimony has been provided on the practices by the monopolist, which in my view have placed a technical and financial stranglehold on the technology industry. Mr. McNealy and Mr. Barksdale and others that have come before me have done a good job of presenting the issues to the Committee. I support their conclusions that the software industry needs government intervention. I support their requests for strong enforcement of antitrust laws.

I would like to reaffirm their case, that innovation will occur when there is a competitive environment free of monopolistic practices.

Open source software arose because of a lack of alternatives that allowed the individual to choose the best tool for the job. Over the past 5 years, projects created by Red Hat and the open source community have become solutions of choice in areas of standards-based Internet software development, areas that the monopolist does not yet control.

The growth of the Linux operating system is an example of this acceptance. The Apache web server is another, it now holds a market-leading position.

However, the Internet browser, desktop operating system and office productivity software are areas that have continued to be influenced by one vendor alone.

One of the reasons I am. so deeply troubled by the consent decree in this case is that it seems to run counter to things that are fundamental to our identity as Americans. We value fair play, ethical competition, abiding by the rules and fostering innovation. The consent decree throws all of this away. It acknowledges that my competitor has broken the law; that through these violations it has built one of the most formidable businesses in the world. Yet the consent decree does little to prevent future misconduct. I feel if the antitrust laws are not enforced, the will and spirit of the true innovators will suffer.

Lengthy legal critiques of the consent decree are already on record. In the interest of time I will not subject you to more this morning. I am sure you've heard enough legal arguments in considering this topic. Rather, I want to make a few key points:

First, their growing monopoly power has seriously warped the technology market. Now that my competitor is a convicted monopolist, the world can see in the public record what those in technology companies have known for years: they don't compete fairly, they use their dominance in one market to dominate others, and they stifle innovation in the name of competition. The only way to stop this—to restore fairness to the market—is a settlement of this case that denies the monopolist the fruits of its past actions and provides remedial measures on the monopolist for its violations of the law.

Second, the consent decree as it stands today, falls far short of this requirement. Given the monopolist's history of skating up to the edge, or over the edge, in not fully complying with prior settlements, it will take very strong measures to change their behavior. In the words of Massachusetts Attorney General Thomas F. Reilly, commenting on the consent decree: "Five minutes after any agreement is signed with Microsoft, they'll be thinking of how to violate the agreement. They're predators. They crush their competition. They crush new ideas. They stifle innovation. That's what they do."

Microsoft is deeply concerned about open source software and has already making overtures on how it will use dominance rather than technical expertise to crush it.

The CEO of the monopolist said, quote, "Linux is a cancer that attaches itself in an intellectual property sense to everything it touches."

The head of the monopolist's Windows Platform Group has similar beliefs: He said publicly, quote, "Open source is an intellectual property destroyer. I can't imagine something that could be worse than this for the software business." He goes on further to say, "I'm an American, I believe in the American way. I worry if the government encourages open source, and I don't think we've done enough education of policymakers to understand the threat."

In my view, the consent decree should create a level playing field between Windows and Linux. Because of their comments, and their past actions, I believe the current consent decree is not strong enough. They will circumvent it.

Third, we have all heard of the Digital Divide. It's the gap in information and computing access between the haves and have nots in our society. As many states struggle with declining revenues, I believe these shortfalls will have a material impact on the public funding of K–12 and higher education. The path to the development of an information economy can not be limited to a sole supplier, who in my view has seen education up to this point, relative to its financial position as a market—not as a responsibility. I believe the lack of choices and high recurring costs is in part responsible for this growing chasm between the two Americas.

I'm involved with North Carolina Central University—an historically black university that cannot afford the monopolist's restrictive licenses and forced upgrades. I see this sad experience in schools throughout our country. Walk the halls of schools in East Roxbury, MA or Snow Hill, NC and question how we can expect, as a nation, to improve the future for our youth when schools must allocate 30–40% of their IT budget for software and hardware upgrades. Provided choice, these same dollars could be put into teacher training and acquiring more technology.

The Chinese government understands this. The French and German governments as well. They have stated that proprietary software will not be used to develop government and educational infrastructure.

But the monopolist has more than 90% of the desktop operating system market and more than 70% of the Internet browser market. What choices do our schools have? What choices do our citizens have? As the monopolist extends its monopoly into additional markets, largely unfettered by the legal system and apparently immune to the consequences of their actions—the Digital Divide widens.

Biologists know that an unbalanced ecosystem, one dominated by a single species, is more vulnerable to collapse. I think we're seeing this today. Under the consent decree, it will continue and probably get worse.

In America, history has taught us that there is no mechanism more logical and efficient and than a free and open market. Our competitor's illegal monopolistic actions have significantly reduced the open market in information technology. I believe that in extreme cases like this, it is the role of the government to step in and restore balance.

Thank you.

Statement of Hon. Jeff Sessions, a U.S. Senator from the State of Alabama

I am troubled by the decision of Committee, acting in its official capacity, to send a transcript of this hearing to the federal district court that will determine the outcome of this pending litigation. By taking the apparently unprecedented step of sending a transcript of a hearing on pending litigation to the judge that is deciding the case, this Committee may have unintentionally traversed the critical boundary between attempting to inform the court and attempting to influence it.

The Constitution vests the legislative power in the Congress, Article I, § 1, the executive power in the President, Article II, § 1, and the judicial power in the Supreme Court and lower federal courts, Article III, § 1. Thus, Congress has the power to make law pursuant to its enumerated powers, the President has the power to enforce these laws, and the courts have the separate power to "say what the law is"—"to rule on cases . . . to decide them," *Marbury v. Madison*, 5 U.S. (1 Cranch) 137, 177 (1803); *Plaut v. Spendthrift Farm, Inc.*, 514 U.S. 211, 218 (1995).

The separation of powers principle not only outlines the distinct spheres of operation of the three branches of government but also guides the branches in their dealings with each other. It is crystal clear that the Framers of our Constitution intended to have a judiciary that is independent of Congress. The provision for judges to hold office during good behavior in Article III, § 1, for example, was said by Alexander Hamilton to constitute an "excellent barrier to the encroachments and oppressions of the representative body." THE FEDERALIST NO. 78, at 465 (Hamilton) (Clinton Rossiter ed;, 1961). Thus, with respect to this case, Congress, the Senate, and this Committee, should defer to the court to decide the case by exercising its independent judgement. A publicized congressional hearing and a transcript submission to the court can only be perceived as an attempt to create for senators a status at a Tunney hearing that neither the court nor the Tunney Act permits.

While the Tunney Act provides that a district court should accept comments from the public on a proposed antitrust settlement agreement, it does not provide for any role by the legislative branch in such a hearing. *See* Pub. L. No. 93–528 (1974). Indeed, the Congressional Research Service has informed me that it has found "no instances in which any comments—whether Hearing transcripts, summaries of Hearing transcripts, or other written communications—were sent to" the district court in a Tunney Act hearing. Congressional Research Service, Memorandum 2 (Dec. 18, 2001).

While any senator may file comments on a proposed settlement agreement as a private citizen, it infringes upon the separation of powers principle for the Senate or this Committee officially to do so. It is the litigants and the public that inform the court in a Tunney Act hearing, not the Congress. *See* Pub. L. No. 93–528. For this Committee to submit its views on the merits of pending litigation creates the appearance of an attempt to influence the Article III federal court in the exercise of its independent judicial power.

In addition to my constitutional concern, I have an underlying prudential concern. This transcript will include several statements from Senators opining on the merits of the Microsoft settlement agreement. A case such as this one involves a complex body of law and a extraordinary amount of evidence. Neither I nor, to the best of my knowledge, any other member of this Committee or of the Senate has had an opportunity to thoroughly review the law and the facts of this case. Consequently, our opinion with respect to this non-legislative matter is worth no more than that of any other reasonably informed citizen who may submit information to the court. There is no legitimate rationale for any court to give more weight to our opinions, whether stamped with the imprimatur of this Committee or not, than to the opinions of others. Accordingly, I respectfully object to the Chairman and Ranking Member's decision, without a vote of the Committee, to submit on behalf of the Committee, a copy of the transcript of this hearing to the district court.

WILLIAM H. SORRELL
ATTORNEY GENERAL

J. WALLACE MALLEY, JR.
DEPUTY ATTORNEY GENERAL

WILLIAM E. GRIFFIN
CHIEF ASST. ATTORNEY GENERAL

TEL.: (802) 828-3171
FAX: (802) 828-2154
TTY: (802) 828-3665
CIVIL RIGHTS: (802) 828-3657

http://www.state.vt.us/atg

STATE OF VERMONT
OFFICE OF THE ATTORNEY GENERAL
109 STATE STREET
MONTPELIER
05609-1001

September 20, 2001

Steven A. Ballmer
Chief Executive Officer
Microsoft
One Microsoft Way
Redmond, WA 98052-6399
Fax No. 425-936-7329

Dear Mr. Ballmer:

In 1998, the Department of Justice and a significant number of state attorneys general filed a lawsuit alleging that Microsoft had monopoly power in the operating system market and that the company had engaged in illegal predatory practices to maintain this monopoly. Our states are not parties to the pending litigation. However, we have a continuing interest in issues relevant to the litigation.

Today we write to you to express our support for concerns raised by the states and the Department of Justice in the litigation. We add our voices to those calling on Microsoft to remedy the antitrust problems that are now evident. We take this action for three reasons.

First, as a result of the trial record, we now have the ability to review a complete record of evidence concerning Microsoft's activities over the past several years to maintain its monopoly in the operating system market. Second, the district court's finding of monopoly maintenance was confirmed unanimously by the United States Court of Appeals for the District of Columbia Circuit. Finally, given our understanding of Microsoft's new Windows XP operating system, which is about to be released, we are concerned that aspects of this new product may lead to further erosion of competition in various software markets.

We are concerned that Windows XP may involve additional unlawful attempts by Microsoft to maintain its operating system monopoly. Notwithstanding the notable technological achievements imbedded into some of the products and services offered by Windows XP, Microsoft may have constructed this new product without due regard for relevant legal rulings, and without due regard for other issues involving consumer choice and consumer privacy.

Steven A. Ballmer
Page 2

September 20, 2001

Moreover, there are many state governmental agencies currently using existing versions of Windows, and there are significant expressions of concern that Microsoft will be in a position to withdraw support for products currently in use in favor of Windows XP.

We agree with our colleagues, the litigating states and the federal government, that any anti-competitive aspects of Windows XP should be addressed. As the Court of Appeals succinctly stated, the remedy must, to the extent possible, "unfetter [the] market from anticompetitive conduct, ... and ensure that there remain no practices likely to result in monopolization in the future." We therefore are supportive of efforts of the litigating states and the Department of Justice to incorporate Windows XP into the remedy phase of the remanded case.

Sincerely,

William H. Sorrell
Vermont Attorney General

On behalf of himself and:

Mark Pryor
Arkansas Attorney General

G. Steven Rowe
Maine Attorney General

Mike McGrath
Montana Attorney General

Phillip McLaughlin
New Hampshire Attorney General

Sheldon Whitehouse
Rhode Island Attorney General